THE STRATEGIC LEAN OFFICE

Where to start and how to get there

Neil R. Trivedi

MAPLE
PUBLISHERS

The Strategic Lean Office

Author: Neil Trivedi

Copyright © Neil Trivedi (2022)

The right of Neil Trivedi to be identified as author of this work has been asserted by the author in accordance with section 77 and 78 of the Copyright, Designs and Patents Act 1988.

First Published in 2022

ISBN 978-1-915164-44-5 (Paperback)
978-1-915164-45-2 (Ebook)

Book cover design and Book layout by:

White Magic Studios
www.whitemagicstudios.co.uk

Published by:

Maple Publishers
1 Brunel Way,
Slough,
SL1 1FQ, UK
www.maplepublishers.com

CONTENTS

Foreword

Lean improvement traditionally focusses on improving manufacturing operations. Whilst this is the logical place to start for many organisations, it by-passes the cause of many of the issues we see in the factory – the office processes. Decisions and data are made and created at a different time and place to factory operations. However, their impact is seen later in the process – or value stream, the factory. It can be argued that this at the start of the process and can have far more significant impact on operations rather than what happens in the factory itself.

This workshop manual for the improvement of business processes has been created from the experience of the author through 3 global Lean deployments across the "office" side of manufacturing organisations. It is intended to support teams that are starting their journey to deploy Lean in their business processes and take Lean into the office. It progresses through the 8 -step approach for improving business processes, from the alignment to business strategy, selection of the key process through to implementation, sustaining the improvements and creating a "self-healing process" through the end state Lean management systems and process visualisation. This in turn leads to a culture of continuous improvement across the entity.

I'd like to give my thanks to John Bicheno for his Lean mentorship over the 20 years I have known him, Peter Watkins as my manager who developed me the most, Frank Devine for his coaching and detailed review of this book, Ian Capewell and Martin Lunn for their support and sense of humour during our time working together and most of all to my wife Lesley for her support and patience to allow me to write this book.

Introduction

The aim of this book is to enable office teams to improve their business processes through a structured approach. It demonstrates the link between strategy and improvement activity. It shows the link between leadership and strategy with improvement activity and tackles the challenges and pitfalls of Lean change in the office

The purpose of this book is to provide the detailed steps to enable teams to decide their priority processes and improve these using the 8-step method as a framework for improvement. It illustrates the challenges and pitfalls of change and enable teams to deploy countermeasures to ensure success. It considers the best way to enable the improvement to succeed through embedding ways to ensure success through the early use of countermeasures – set up to succeed before the start. It concludes by linking the Lean tools in the office to the lean daily management system to provide a sustainable system that enables teams to start the process of continuous improvement.

Strategy Deployment

Introduction

The first part of business planning and improvement to consider when starting on a journey of Lean improvement is the alignment of the improvement activity to the business strategy. Quite often the Lean improvement starts because of a business objective. "This is the year we are doing lean" was a quote I heard at a company I visited. When we discussed what was involved to deploy Lean, their reaction to the work involved was one of surprise, they had not considered the link to strategy important nor the investment in resources required to do it properly. The question around strategy is important as it prompts the organisation to look inward and first check that one exists and is live in the organisation. Often the strategy has been created and left in the bottom drawer to collect dust.

Why is strategy important? after all we are "doing Lean" not strategy deployment. The reason is that Lean is not a strategy creation tool nor a market analysis tool. Lean is an improvement method that encompasses strategy deployment but can only help improve what you have already in the direction you have set. It's no good producing goods or services very effectively and efficiently if no-one wants to buy them! As a result, it important to check the business strategy and then align the improvement activity to the strategies key objectives.

> There are 3 key elements to starting a business process improvement activity.
>
> 1. Understand customer value – here represented by the kano model
> 2. Define and understand the link between business strategy and the improvement activity
> 3. Be able to answer the "WIFM" question – "*what's in this for me?*".

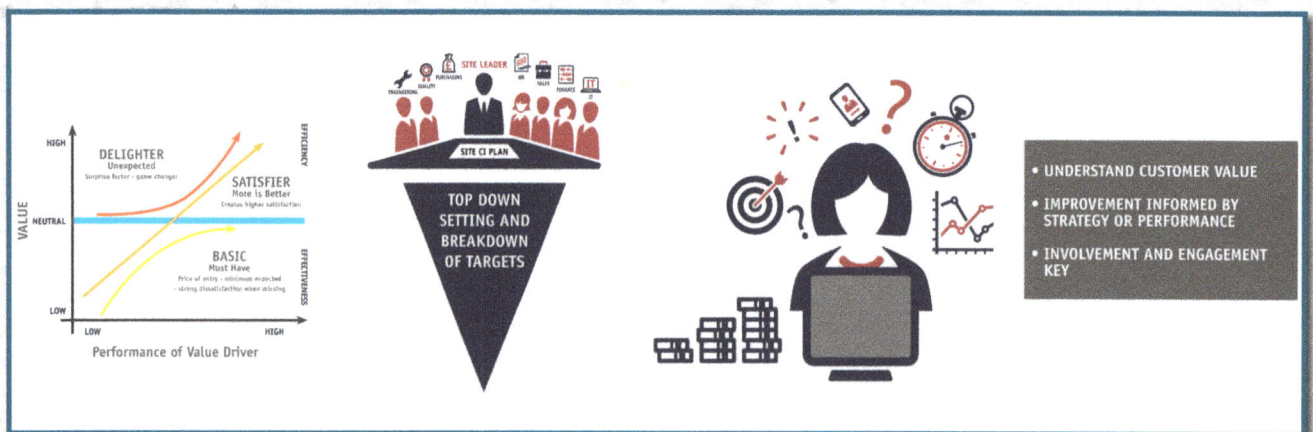

Understanding Customer Value

Lean business process improvement is about removing the wastes and issues that prevent the flow of value – as defined by the customer. The first step is to understand what value means. The Kano model explores value in several dimensions

The Kano Model

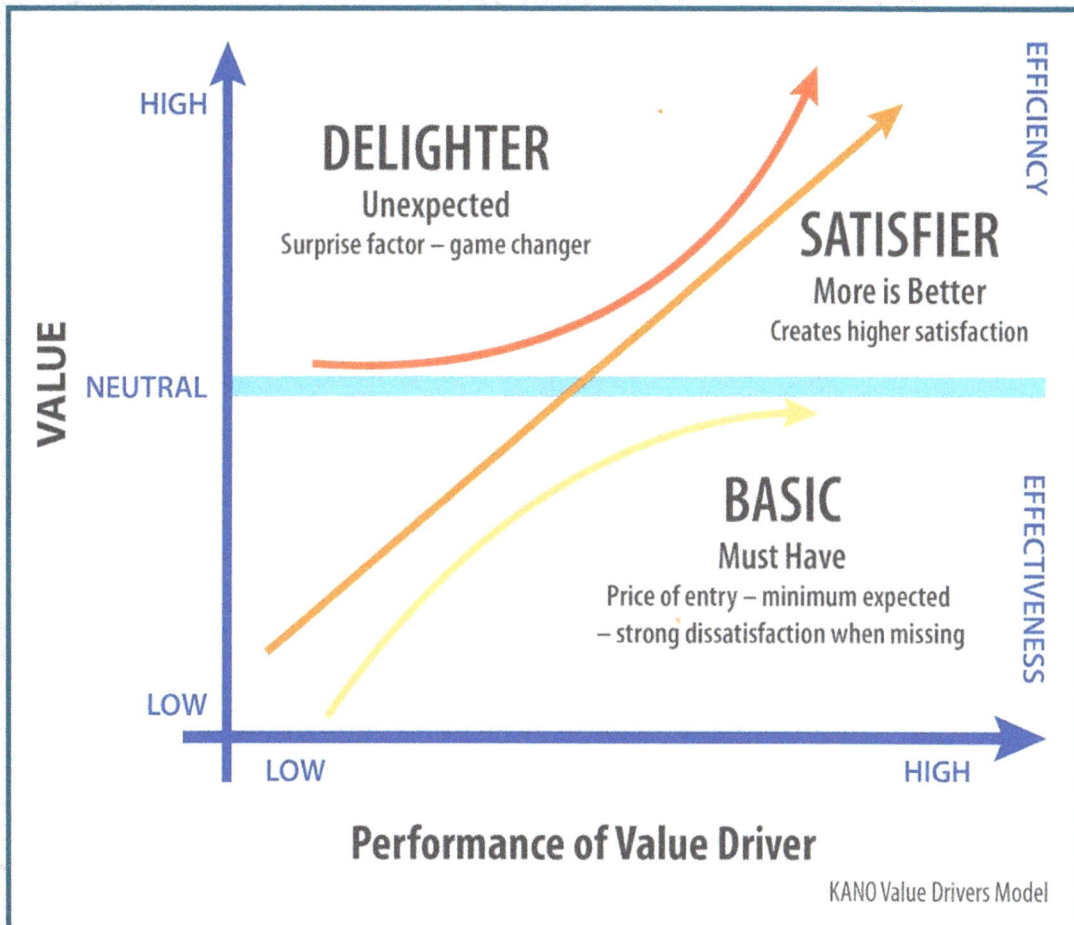

Kano et al 1984

There are 3 attributes of the Kano model that help define value

1. Basic needs that you must have – the user expects the qualities and will be dissatisfied if they are not fulfilled. For example, a clean hotel room, with air con, TV, and free Wi-Fi.

2. Satisfier – The more of an attribute that is present the happier the customer will be. For example, fewer servicing costs for a car, bigger portions of food, less waiting time than anticipated.

3. Delighter – These are unexpected attributes that exceed user expectation. These are sometime called order winners. For example, very quick counter service, extras in the hotel room, free items related to a purchase and continuous software updates on a Tesla.

A simple example of the Kano model applied to hire cars used in the author's workshops

	Attribute 1	Attribute 2	Attribute 3	Attribute 4	Attribute 5
Basic	Clean	Fuelled	Model requested	Minimal queue/wait	Minimal queue at return
Satisfier	Recent model car	Pre-paid fuel	Higher model provided	Pre check-in and instant pick up	No queue at return
Delighter	Brand new car	Free fuel, no need to re-fuel	Free choice of car	Car delivered to you	Return at departure terminal

The application of the Kano model to hire cars shows how value levels can be understood in service. One hidden element of the kano model is how delighter and standard features transition over time to become basic needs. A great example of this is air conditioning in cars. In the 70's and 80's this was an additional feature either attracting extra cost as an accessory or only available on top – end cars. Now if we get into a rental car and there is no air con/climate control/zonal heating, we will refuse the car!

The question for your organisation is what are your customer basic needs, satisfiers, and delighters?

Complete the following table for your organisation:

Steps:

1. Brainstorm customer value attributes using post-its
2. Categorise in the 3 attributes
3. Prioritise the top 5 according to impact on the attribute

	Attribute 1	Attribute 2	Attribute 3	Attribute 4	Attribute 5
Basic					
Satisfier					
Delighter					

These categorised value attributes will help to understand what helps value flow and what is "waste" as we progress through the business process improvement workshop.

Strategy deployment and process improvement

A lot of business strategies are rarely used, are only shared with the executive teams in an organisation or it are too abstract to make any sense to employees.

Strategies fail for 5 key reasons:

Why?	Reason
People cannot implement what they do not know.	Communication gaps
People do not implement properly what they do not understand.	Knowledge gaps
People do not implement what they are not committed to.	Lack of commitment
People give up on a strategy, the implications of which have not been anticipated	Lack of need or compelling argument for change
Leadership overlooks the 'How' of executing a strategy	It's too much in the clouds and not based on the reality of the situation

Typical causes are insufficient time and focus on the process of deploying and delivering the strategy

What is the difference between a good and bad strategy?

Good Strategy	Bad strategy
Comes from fresh insight into your strengths, weaknesses, opportunities, and threats	Urges achievement of a goal – nothing else
Is honest in identifying challenges	Tries to meet conflicting goals and avoids making hard choices
Develops a cohesive approach to overcome the challenges	Is wishful thinking
Identifies what to do and what to stop	Problems are ignored – a failure to face the challenge
It differentiates you from the crowd	Impractical strategic objectives

Top-down setting and breakdown of targets

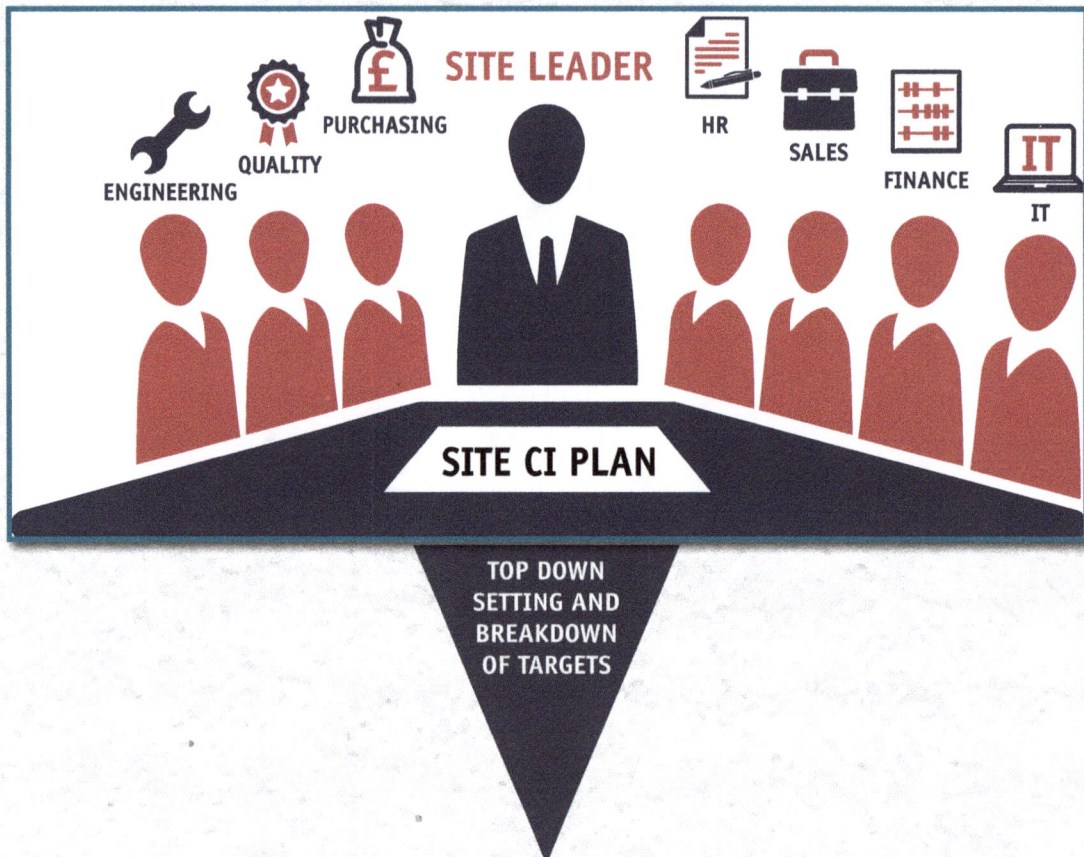

Converting this strategy into meaningful objectives for the team and team members is called policy deployment.

Policy deployment directs people to do what they should do, not what they want to do by:

- Aligning activities to the strategic vision.
- Delivering the business strategy by aligning employees, functions, and divisions to the business goals.
- Focussing on the few business-critical issues by establishing clear gaps between goals and current state performance.
- Creating ownership, buy-in and commitment through the involvement of everyone in the 'catchball' process.

Policy deployment provides a means to bring functions together by aligning objectives. It challenges 'Silo' thinking (people only thinking about their own department or function rather than the wider business context). At its heart is Plan, Do, Check, Act thinking

Leadership teams need to create a site continuous improvement plan together. The team should be cross functional and represent all the key processes within the organisation.

To succeed, Lean must be supported from the top of the organisation, anything less and it will not be sustained. Leaders need to maintain focus so that it remains top of their team's and people's agenda. After all, "what's important to my boss is important to me".

Policy deployment aligns department objectives to business goals

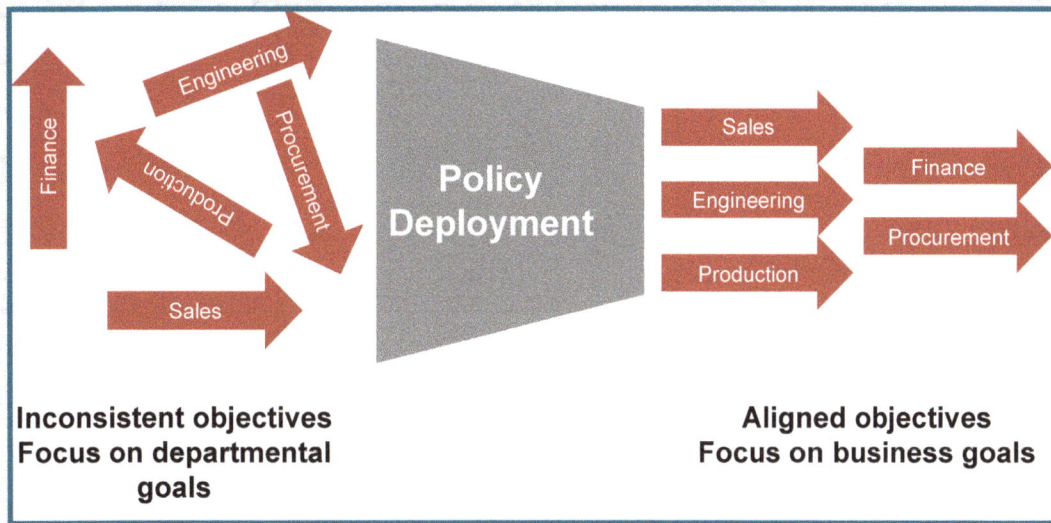

Inconsistent objectives
Focus on departmental goals

Policy Deployment

Aligned objectives
Focus on business goals

Companies are typically organised by function or department. As a result, they may become more biased towards their own functional objectives rather than "the greater good". For example, purchasing have a cost reduction target which they achieve through bulk buying. They achieved their cost saving; however, the stock took so long to use it went obsolete and suffered quality issues. During covid, one organisation lost control of its purchasing rigour and ended up with surplus raw materials which quickly became obsolete. Furthermore, prior to covid different raw materials (SKUs), had been allowed to proliferate, further exacerbating the situation during covid. Policy deployment derives department objectives from the business strategy, so everyone is working towards the same goals.

Bottom-up process improvement focuses on small daily improvements

We often think about our work as a combination or collection of tasks. All work belongs to a process. One of the first steps is getting the team to recognise and prioritise their processes.

On the other side, ideas for improvement also need to be generated "bottom up" from each team's Lean daily management system. Typically, these will be focussed on small daily improvements that the team can make for itself but will also naturally include what others can do to support the team. Improvement ideas from the teams can also include key processes. This may arise due to the challenges and issues with a certain process which are felt at the front line. These processes are typically cross-functional, so need the support of the multi-disciplinary leadership team to get resources and support for the improvement activity. Improving these processes can be just as important as those relating to the strategy

– it will help bring people along the improvement journey as it starts to answer the

"what's in this for me question"

Lean Daily Management System: This is a collection of process control and validation methods which manage and improve the business process. Typically, it will include process visualisation, Leader's Standard Work, problem solving all knitted together through a tiered accountability system.

An example of a team's issue brainstorm:

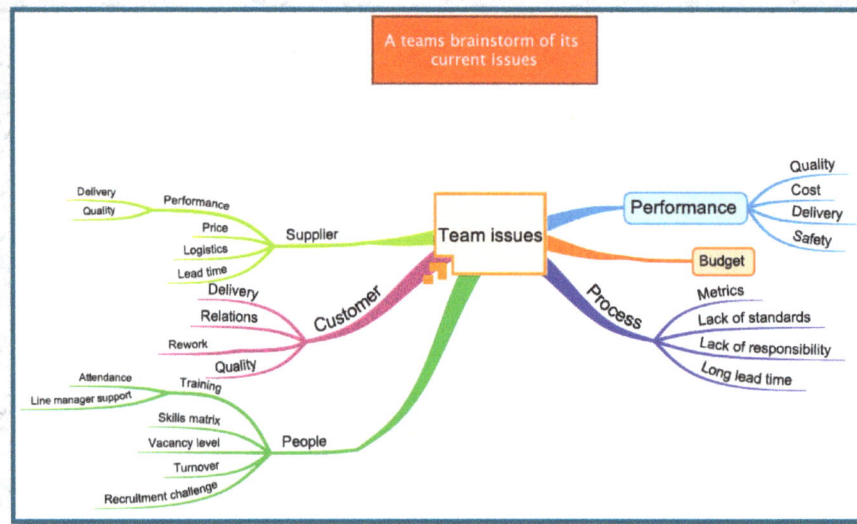

Example from one of the author's workshops

This mind map shows the typical types of issues a team could generate at a high level. For each of the issues a specific problem statement would need to be developed to illustrate the link between the problem and the process.

What's in this for me?

In the background of every workshop, the attendees are thinking "how much work will this generate and why should I participate"? The *what's in this for me question?*

It's easy to appreciate why a top-down approach is the logical first step to the improvement journey in business processes. A cascade for the senior team aligned to the business strategy is the first step many companies take in strategic deployment and improvement. However, at the start of any improvement journey, one question always emerges – how do we make sure this happens and sustained? This question should really be the first in any change journey.

To initiate any change initiative a certain amount of time and resources must be dedicated to the project to enable the analysis to be performed, benefits to be identified and actions to be completed. Rather like starting up a steam engine where you must fire the boiler, fill the tank, and finally get steam up before the engine will move. Unlike the factory where work stops when you walk away, in the office (and for those who work in business processes), the work continues in the background. The emails add up, the messages continue, the phone and the tacit conversations that were going to happen are collected for your return. The people involved, may legitimately ask, why should I invest my time and effort in this project when all I am going to go back to is a mountain of work? *"What's in it for me?"*

So how can this problem be avoided? The first step is the logical deployment of objectives to the team. This sets the high-level purpose for individuals. The next step is to really understand and resolve the daily frustrations of the team and work to resolve them as part of the improvement activity. You may think that it is difficult to elicit feedback from the team. However, it is more often the case that there are more issues to resolve than paper to capture them on! So, the buy-in process for the team starts by simply recording the issues as they are raised in the workshop and then including them in the waste analysis and action plan in steps 5 and 7 of the 8-step improvement process respectively. Moving to the later steps of action planning, delegating some of these actions to the people who raised the issue closes the accountability loop and places the solution in the hands of the person who benefits the most from the action and who raised it in the first place.

The benefits of creating a Lean system that generates small daily improvements as well as big ticket process improvements is that the total of both improvement methods will be greater than the sum of the individual approaches.

Step change improvement projects run a risk at the sustaining stage if not they are not supported by the lean daily management system approach

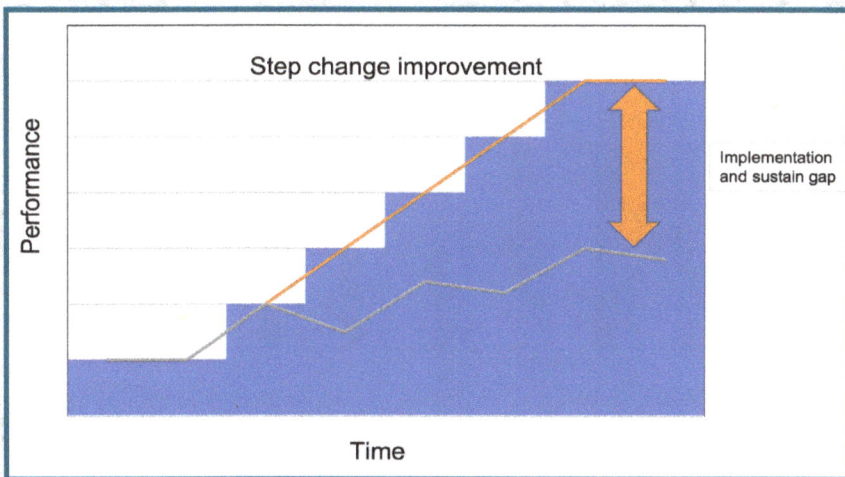

The Lean Daily Management System has many features. One aspect is the ability to include regular reviews of small projects or improvement to ensure that they get implemented – this helps drive daily continuous improvement.

The Lean daily management system provides the opportunity for small daily improvements. This system supports the implementation and sustaining of step change process improvement projects.

Small daily improvements

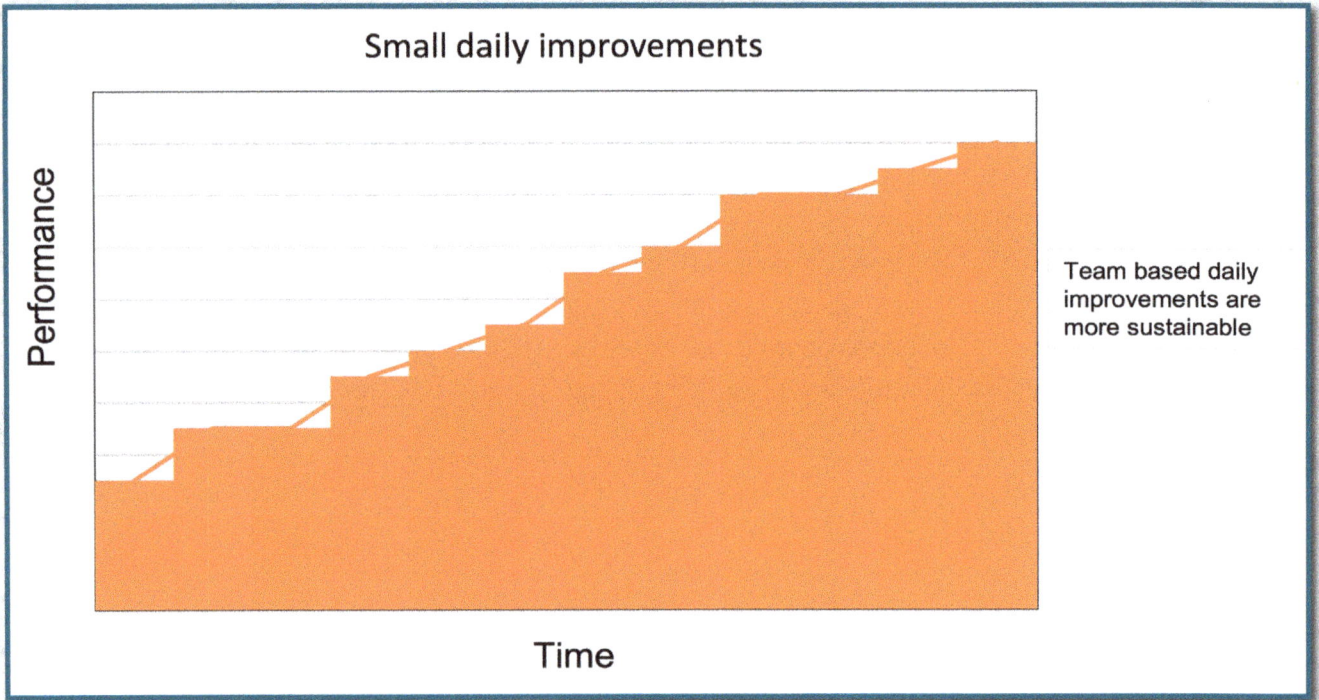

Performance / Time

Team based daily improvements are more sustainable

The combined benefits of small daily improvement and step change projects are greater than the sum, as a culture of improvement has been achieved through the lean daily management system

Project and daily improvements

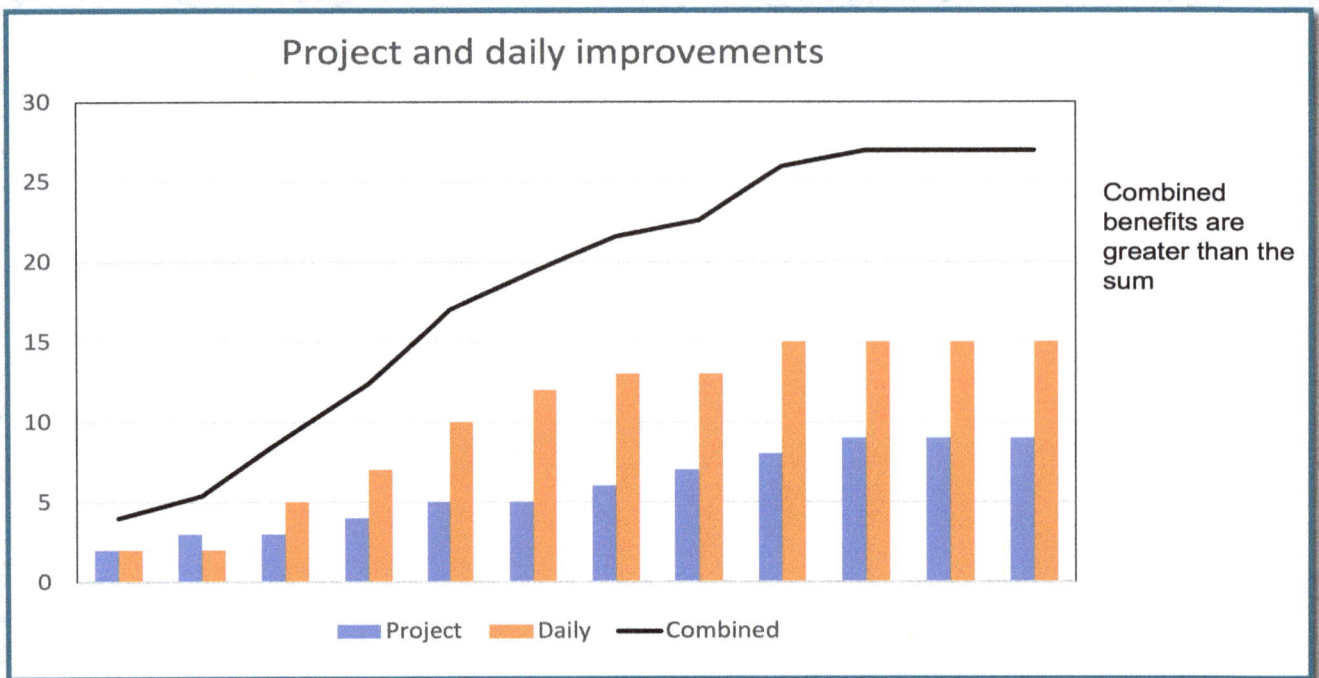

Combined benefits are greater than the sum

Legend: Project — Daily — Combined

Why does this happen?

One of the first typical activities for a Lean deployment is value stream mapping (VSM). This generates several different projects across the value stream. Typically, a proportion of these are smaller team-based projects which require local implementation. As the VSM is being managed as a project the line of sight to the implementation actions can be distant. So less critical actions get pushed the back of the list and forgotten. These represent the smaller CI type activities.

Lean daily management is a structured system which checks the performance of the key processes in a team and highlights both performance gaps and helps the team identify and deliver smaller continuous improvement projects. So, the team is set up for improvement.

When significant change projects are implemented, an amount of project work falls of the individual teams to do. Teams who already have the Lean daily management system in place have a ready-made mature process for delivering small projects. This experience means they pick up other smaller parts and have the motivation to complete tasks without having to be convinced. Furthermore, these actions from the step change project provoke further ideas for local team improvement.

Step 1 Define the need

Select the process to improve from strategic objectives

	NAME	PROCESS			
		A	B	C	D
1	....	✓		✓	
2	....	✓	✓	✓	
3	....	✓			✓
4	....	✓			
5	....		✓		

PRIORITISE PROCESSES VS OBJECTIVES

A simple matrix can be used to score the impact of each process on achieving business objectives.

There are 2 ways to determine what should be improved.

1. Top-down targets from business strategy – typically breakthrough targets devolved from the top of the business

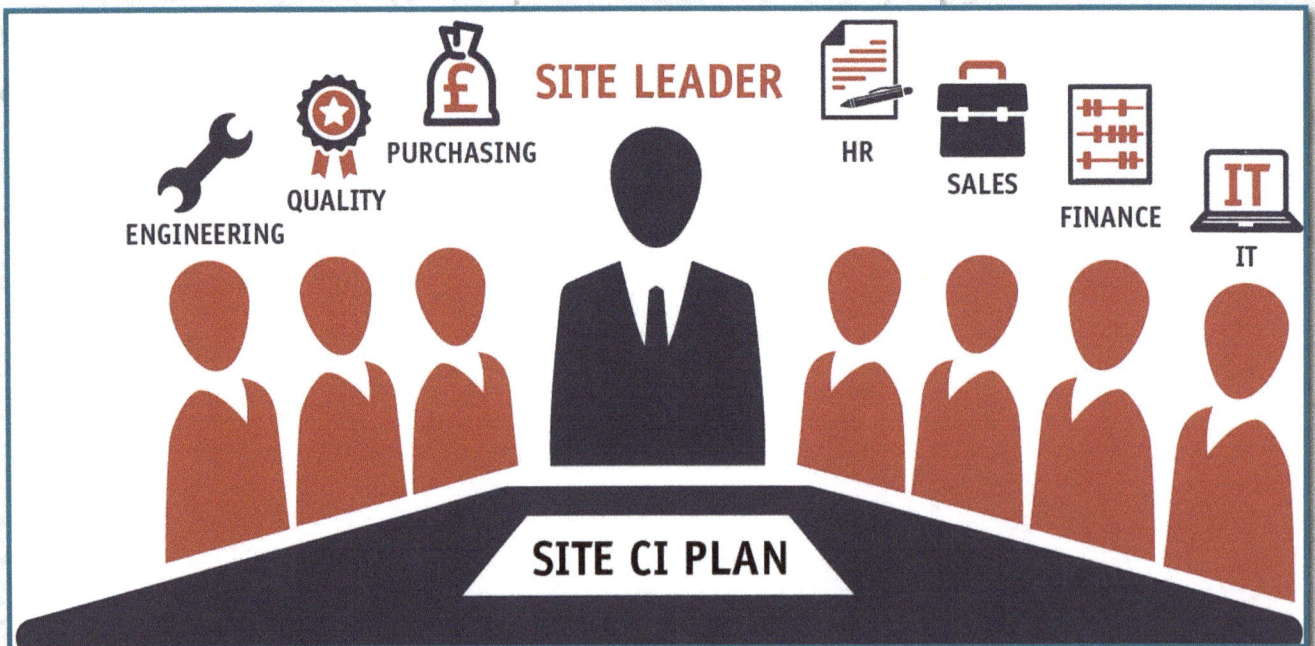

SITE LEADER

ENGINEERING QUALITY PURCHASING HR SALES FINANCE IT

SITE CI PLAN

2. And/or bottom-up improvement through the monitoring of results

It's all too easy to choose processes to improve that are not a priority or will not deliver business benefits, so it's important to focus on business targets or projects that are bottom-up ideas to gain engagement.

Ideally the main improvement activity must be aligned to a CI plan or business objectives. The alignment to key business activities and direction is important to demonstrate and maintain. More random ideas or favourite projects have less chance of success

Leadership sponsorship and support ensure success. Leaders are the only ones able to provide resources and time for improvement. This Support comes with consistent alignment to business objectives – the site CI plan.

1. Creating a top-down CI plan

There are several key inputs that enable the creation of the site CI plan. Typically, a leadership team will look backwards to do a business performance review to see where there are gaps and opportunities. A mature Lean organisation will review last year's CI Plan to see how effective it was, highlight any projects that were missed, need to be rolled over or rebased for the new year. Alignment to business strategy is essential as the CI plan can be used to drive actions to deliver these objectives. Looking outside the business, a review of customer and supplier situations may highlight wider business issues. A PEST analysis – Political, Economic, Social and Technological 2x2 matrix and a SWOT analysis – Strengths, Weaknesses, Opportunities and Threats 2x2 matrix will help cover all aspects of a wider economic review and capture anything else pertinent to the CI plan.

A structured approach to CI planning for a site will yield far more effective results – the P of PDCA. The targets are owned at a local level through the CI planning process

Creating bottom-up improvement ideas:

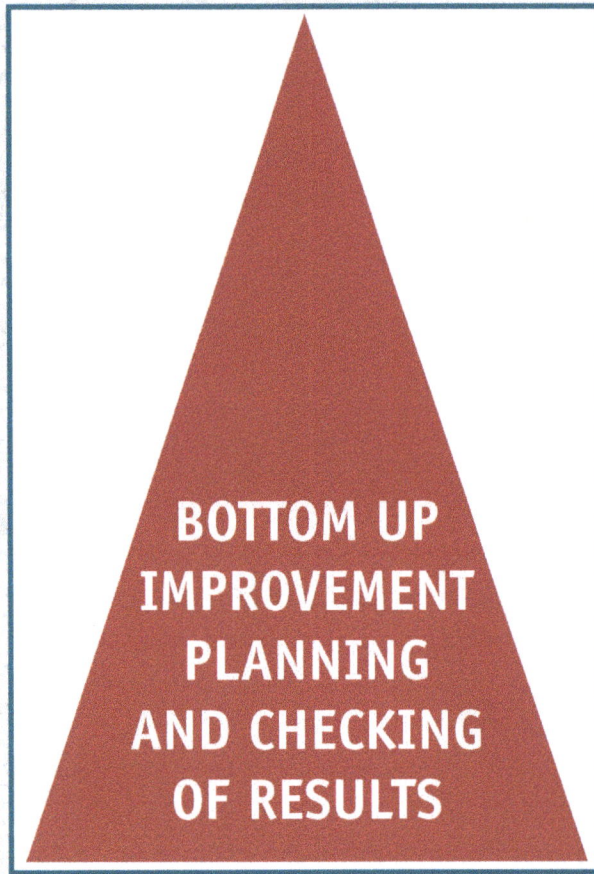

BOTTOM UP IMPROVEMENT PLANNING AND CHECKING OF RESULTS

Quite often at the start of the Lean journey, ideas for improvement come from the top or are generated through technical improvements which require investment. A mature Lean system has a foundation of improvement generated by the team doing the work on a day-to-day basis. It's important that the overall system – the Lean Daily Management System has elements to support and coach ideas from the front line.

Each team within a business should be operating the Lean Daily Management System. Within this system ideas will be generated for improvement. These fall into 3 categories:

1. Small improvements that can be implemented by the team (online)
2. Small improvements that require external support to completed (offline)
3. Larger process improvements that need leadership sponsorship to implement.

Clearly actions that fall under 1) should be easily achieved by the team with only occasional coaching support required by leadership. In a mature Lean organisation these types of action should not require leadership intervention, however for those of us still on the journey they may need some form of leadership intervention. With actions that fall under 2) which are outside the team and beyond their span of control, leadership support is more likely to be required to facilitate, motivate, and prioritise actions within other teams and their leaders.

For the larger process improvements which will need resources, coaching and maybe some direction, leadership sponsorship and ownership is the key to success. These are the types of improvements that need to be included in the CI plan.

How do you select the process to improve?

In the ideal world in a mature system process to improve would be clearly identified through the business strategy, however many organisations need a place to start. The first gentle step is to link the process (improvement) to a strategic objective for example strategic objective - improve cash flow and reduce the lead time of the accounts receivable process. Some processes are quite straightforward to identify and may be hot spots - for example recruitment, accounts payable and month end. Some other processes can be simply a pain. These can be difficult to identify, define and may not exist.

One of the key gaps in strategy deployment is relating the strategy to something that we can change or do differently. The way to make this link is through a simple priority matrix.

This is how it works:

On the vertical add in the strategic objectives, note there is only room for 5 – if you have more then re-prioritise to end up with 5. (Having too many strategic objectives is as bad as having none). On the horizontal add in the key business processes – again it's likely there will be more but prioritise the top 5 again.

Strategic Objectives	Key business Process 1	Key business Process 2	Key Business Process 3	Key Business Process 4	Key Business Process 5
	Sales acquisition	Order to cash	New product development	Supplier development	Accounts receivable
1. Improve sales by 10%	10	7	3	0	0
2. Reduce landfill by 30%	0	7	0	0	0
3. Increase market share in EU by 10%	8	6	7	0	0
4. Develop 3 new products	3	0	10	0	0
5. Improve cash flow	0	8	0	7	9
Total	21	28	20	7	9

Now score each business process out of 10 for its impact on the strategic objectives. Once this is complete, total the columns. The highest column number for the key business process tells us which to prioritise – as it impacts the strategy the most. This makes the link between strategy and improvement planning clear and the basis of the continuous improvement plan for the site or function. In the example it's the order to cash process by a clear margin. However, be aware that, in some cases the choices are not so clear cut and require further discussion to agree the priority process. This method is not definitive so further discussion may occur even with a clear result. In one business we reviewed the HR director changed the scores during a break when everyone was out of the room… so the consensus process had to start again when everyone returned! One way

Frank Devine identified to help reduce the influence of the "senior voice" of status is to ask the leaders to voice their views last of all.

The most important factor is agreement at the end of the discussion.

Improve a process – team-based activity

> Looking at key metrics of a process for example lead time, quality or turnover for example can provide clues for improvement. Even just asking the team for what frustrates them daily can be invaluable.

In a similar way, a team can decide on a process to improve. The team needs to understand its issues as the first step. It needs to take time out to think about its work and what could be made easier as it is easy to get involved in day-to-day work and miss the issues.

You may need to ask the group to brainstorm their issues from strategy, customer, budget, and key measures feedback. They should know their priorities, but you may have to probe to flush them out. For example:

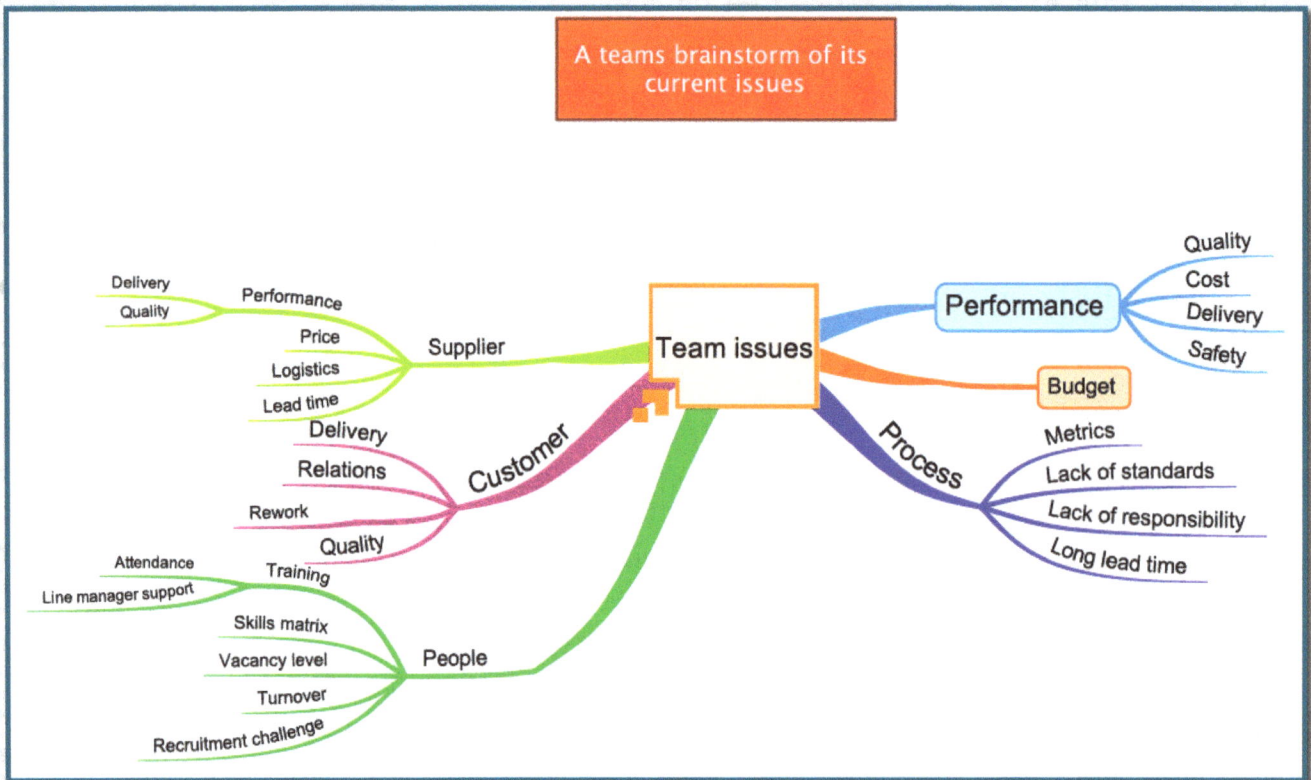

Example from one of the author's workshops

Neil Trivedi

There are a couple of "watch outs" as real life is never that simple:

If the process is cross functional then you will need senior leaders support to mobilise the team. People are often blinkered with their work and will stick to their own remit as defined by their manager so will not "help" offline, so it's important to get all leaders supporting the review with a cross functional process.

In a lot of businesses there will be no real process for some of the work. The process just informally happens. Its difficult to work through this so prompt using the following questions:

"What would you do if there was no real process?"

"What are the things that happen"

"Who is involved?"

The data may not be available to enable you to review the process effectively, so information may be subjective and a matter of opinion rather than fact. Pure consensus can work, especially at the start of the Lean journey but it's better to replace it with fact as soon as possible. Typically, you will find that the process is a collection of activities done by a group of people over a period of time. Just because there are documents or spread sheets to fill out it doesn't mean there is a clear process standard that is repeatable every time in the same way. Often these processes rely on specific individuals to make things happen. When it comes to creating a current state process map, it's difficult!

A better approach may be to jump to future state once you have collected as much data / information as possible about current ways of working.

It is not uncommon to find processes that have not been defined. In one company 25% of their business processes were not defined. We were surprised, only to find that the figure for the next company we worked at was 35%! You must be practical in this situation and review business, location, department, and team business process information:

- Use the knowledge of the team
- Use business indicators/KPIs
- Use customer feedback

Once these issues have been identified and prioritised, align these issues to your business processes. To make sure the effort in improving the process is in the right area for the team, use a matrix of business processes vs issues to prioritise the team process to work on. Gain alignment and support and make a logical decision.

A HR teams' evaluation of its issues mapped against its key processes:

HR Team Issues	Team Process 1 Recruitment	Team Process 2 Payroll	Team Process 3 Training	Team Process 4 Induction	Team Process 5 Grievance
Time taken to recruit a manager	10	0	0	8	0
OT payments late/incorrect	0	10	0	0	0
Low attendance at training	0	0	10	3	0
Low employee satisfaction score	5	8	10	5	10
High turnover	7	1	9	3	10
Total	22	19	29	19	20

Example developed from one of the author's workshops

The table tells us that the key process to review is training as it has the highest score.

In the same way as before, create a matrix on a flipchart, complete the row and column headings and then score each process for impact on the issue. It is always worthwhile to challenge the group on the content and ensure consensus regularly. Consensus is key to future success with the project

Tasks to Complete

- Review the continuous improvement plan to determine which process is next to improve
- If there is no continuous improvement plan, create one.

Outputs from this step

- Clear prioritised process to improve which will impact the business and take a step towards the strategy deployment
- Senior sponsor identified for the process

Step 2 Define the scope

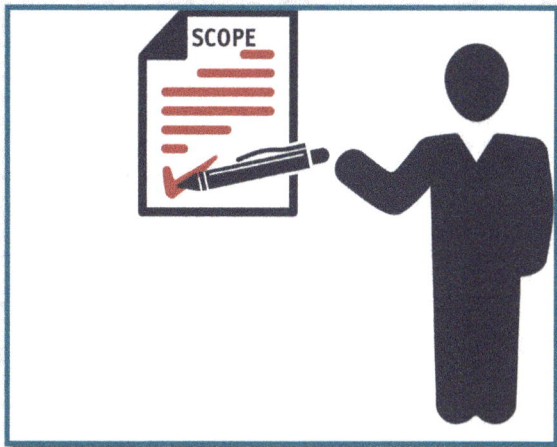

In manufacturing it's easy to see the physical process and its quite well defined. Business processes, however, are more difficult to visualise and identify as they travel through people as well as in and out of systems (which have often never been defined). Therefore, it is even more important to create and agree a scope document to define the process and area for improvement to avoid any confusion, scope creep or exclusion.

Agreeing the scope creates a virtual box around the process

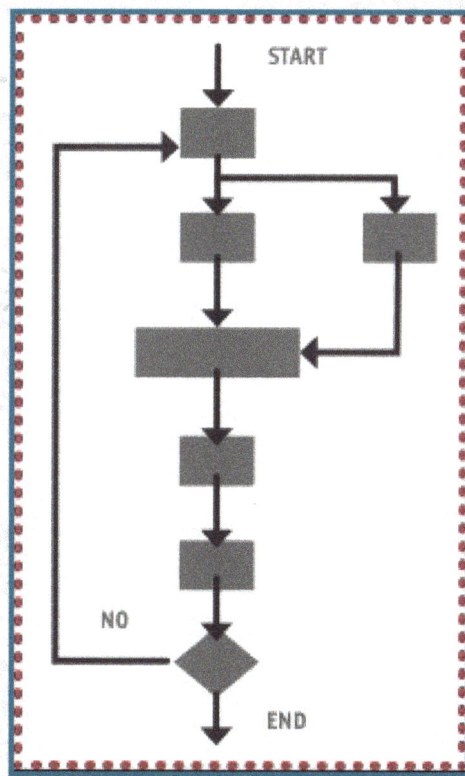

When any improvement project is started its important to define the span of the activity. It is very easy to allow the scope to "creep" i.e., expand to an unmanageable size or on the other hand to shrink so that it will not improve anything.

The scope document is a "getting started" document to enable the team to understand the operating box – both the top and the bottom of the process as well as the width.

As the project moves forward it's important to recognise that the scope may change as you progress through the workshop. This occurs as data and facts emerge about the process during the data collection (step 3) and current state mapping (step 4). These form a base of reality rather than assumptions, guesses and estimations about the process. These new facts and data need to be reflected into the scope document as necessary.

The purpose of the scope document helps determine customer value for the process and understand the purpose of the process. The scope document defines the terms of reference and provides the "operating box" to kick off the process review. Many people make mistake of not scoping out what we are going to do first – think then act rather than PDCA (Plan Do Check Act). The scope document expresses:

- The objectives of the improvement and ensures alignment with business objectives
- Determines the sponsors and the key people who need to be involved in reviewing & improving the process
- Defines the process under review, its start and end as well as its breadth
- Evaluates the risk involved and identifies countermeasures

To complete the scope document, a small team – normally a sub-set of the wider improvement group meet to agree the scope. Typically, this will include the sponsor, subject matter experts and key stakeholders. This session should take between 1-2 hours, but be prepared for a longer session just in case.

The team creates the scope document together

Consensus and involvement of the whole team are key to a good scope document.

Sometimes the process will cross different sites or countries making a face-to-face session difficult or expensive in terms of travel costs and time. So, consider alternatives as follows using Teams or Zoom. Create a draft and hold short 1:1 video conference meeting to review and improve. Follow this up with a presentation to the full group for approval. Ask individuals for input to the scope and consolidate to form a draft for circulation and approval as above. With input from most participants, ownership will increase and therefore more likely to achieve consensus quickly.

The key steps are:

- Get a broad range of inputs to the scope
- Final agreement to the scope before the workshop phase of improvement commences
- Key stakeholders buy-in.
- Provide the group with a template to follow
- Review and improve the scope during the workshop as new facts and data are uncovered from the reality of mapping

Scope document Structure

Important steps	Key points	Reasons
1. Identify sponsor	• Determine who owns the process improvement and who wants it	• To gain leadership support and a licence to "do"
2. Team members	• Identify the process participants	• Gain their expertise of the process
3. Process name/ purpose	• Identify the process and its outputs	• Clarify what the process does/ does not do
4. Process start and end	• Identify the process start and end triggers	• Avoid scope creep, address the right issues
5. Process value	• Identify key customer value attributes	• Focus the team on value
6. Customer and suppliers	• Identify sources of input and output information	• To understand the process boundaries better
7. Business challenge	• Alignment of the workshop to business objectives	• Identify the objectives for the improvement
8. Current performance	• Identify current measures and the performance	• Understand the current gaps in performance and test the alignment of current measures
9. Delivery plan	• Create a time-based plan to deliver the improvements	• Provide confidence to the stakeholders and team of delivery and completion
10. Barriers and counter measures	• Identify what might stop you and develop solutions	• Need to consider wider aspects of improvement

*The team completes the scope document and agrees
the input through consensus*

No-one knows everything about the process, there will be different perceptions and knowledge of what happens. It takes time to reconcile these differences to a common view. Talk through the scope document and highlight hard to do areas

Benefits of scoping

The team activity of scoping helps to identify the team and aligns them to the task. It confirms leadership support for the project and identifies the resources required. It defines the process "operating box" to avoid potential "scope creep" – where projects get larger and larger whilst the workshop is being run. It helps to gain involvement in through discussion and consensus. It provides alignment and clarity of purpose as well as creating a start point for the review

Risks of not scoping

The main danger of not scoping is a lack of business alignment and leadership support. Most business processes are cross functional so the sponsor of the project will rarely cover the breadth of responsibility for the process. In the same way, without scoping there is a risk that incorrect resources and people will be mobilised or more likely missed out and not included. With the process itself, there is a risk the wrong one is identified, or scope creep occurs during the event. All these factors put together increase the risk of failure.

Tasks to complete for this step:

Assemble relevant stakeholders who have a vested interest in the process, it's important to include the sponsor, stakeholders, and subject matter experts. The next step is to work through consensus to complete scope document and circulate to the full team for review and comment and complete final review during working session to gain alignment & consensus.

Output from this step:

At the end of the session a completed and agreed scope, signed off by sponsor is the output.

The Scope Document

Scope Document:		
Process Name:		
Completed By:	**Date:**	
Role	**Description**	**Details**
Sponsor	Determine who owns the process improvement and who wants it	
Team members	Identify the process participants/Subject matter experts/Stakeholders	
Process name/ purpose	Identify the process and its key outputs	
Process value	Determine customer value for the process	
Process start and end	Identify the process start and end triggers	
Customer and suppliers	Identify sources of input and output information	
Business challenge	Alignment of the workshop to business objectives	
Current performance	Identify current measures and the performance	
Delivery plan	Create a time-based plan to deliver the improvements	
Barriers and countermeasures	Identify what might stop you and solutions	

Step 3 Collect the data

3. COLLECT THE DATA RELEVANT TO THE PROCESS		
LEAD TIME (DAYS)	**RESOURCES (HRS)**	**NOTES**
0	2	1 Person for 2hrs
3	4	2 People for 2hrs each
7	8	8 People for 1hr
10	0.5	1 Person for 1/2hr
12	1.5	1 Person for 1.5hrs
17	0.25	1 Person for 1/4hr
49 Days	16.25hrs	

Example developed for one of the author's workshops

The temptation with this step is just to sit at a computer to trawl databases and emails for information. Whilst this approach may yield valuable information, it's the people that operate the process and they need to be involved to get their data and understand their issues.

Go-see to collect the data and speak to the people who work in the process

Once the scope has been agreed and communicated to the team, the next stage is to go and collect the data. This step could take some time, so it is better to start data collection at least 1 month before the main mapping workshop. The reason for starting this step in good time is due to the typical lack of data availability for business processes. In many organisations, the data associated with Lean transformation (like lead times, quality at each activity, cost, and delivery) are not collected as a matter of routine.

To gain a real view of the process and its data it's important to establish the customer value – as described at the start of the book. This value definition enables us to evaluate the right metrics to consider – i.e., ones that drive customer value from a forward-looking perspective.

Once value has been defined then "go-see" and walk the process. Move from step to step to see who, what, why where and when for the process. Discuss the answers to these questions with the process participants and capture their data.

IT is frequently involved in business processes. For systems and workflows assistance may be required from the super-user or IT to help extract Lean data requirements.

Key Steps:

Discuss the different types of data that can be collected with subject matter experts. Make sure a focus is kept on lead time, task time standards and rework. These factors are the determinants of a good process. The shorter the lead time the better the process – you must be good at everything to have a short lead time. Agree with the team what other types of data may be relevant to the process as the data is collected, check alignment to customer value.

Here are some typical types of data to collect:

- Process Activities / Tasks (*the work*)
- Elapsed time (*the time it takes*)
- Resource time (*the manpower needed*)

- Standards, rules, or guidelines (*the framework*)
- Rework or iteration loop (*the waste and frustration*)
- Current Process information examples
- Process Map
- Procedures
- Working Instructions
- Business information systems

Quite often existing information and mind-sets are not aligned with process thinking.

The Kingman Equation – analysis of Lead time

This method of analysis was developed by Sir John Kingman in 1961. It is a method of calculating the expected waiting time for an activity to occur in a queue.

Simple process diagram to illustrate where the Kingman Equation can be applied

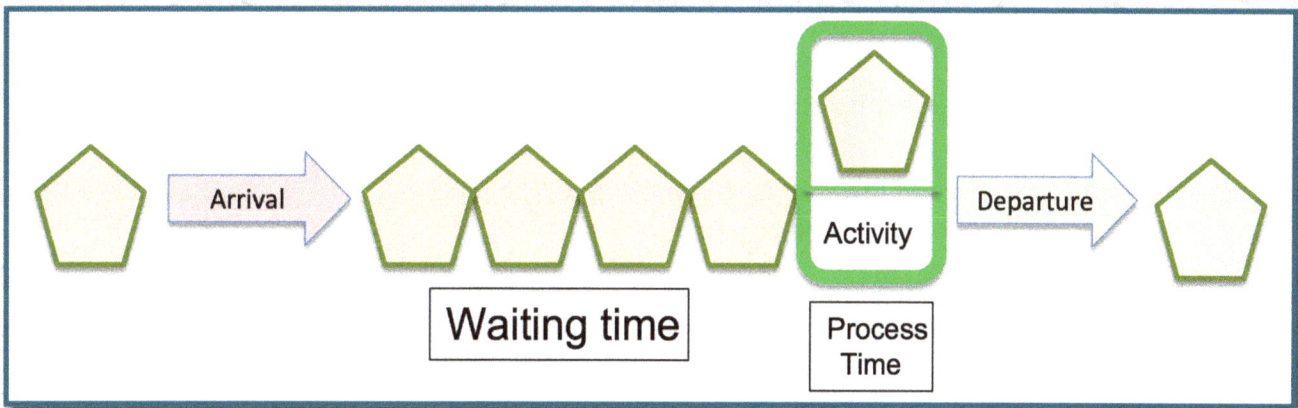

$$E(w) = \left(\frac{p}{1-p}\right) x \left(\frac{Ca^2 + Cp^2}{2}\right) x\, U$$

E(w) = Expected waiting time

P = Utilisation

Ca = Co-efficient of variation of arrival

Cp = Co-efficient of variation for the service

U = Mean time to process one unit

(Kingman 1961)

More simply the equation can be described as:

L = V x U x T

Where:

L = Average lead time

V = Variation, this consists of arrival rate variation and process rate variation

U = Process utilisation

T = Average process time

(Hopp and Spearman 2000)

Key points from Kingman equation:

- Arrival variation: The higher the variation in arrival time the longer the queue. In any system demand variation significantly impacts operations. At one chemical plant we worked at, there were only 4 deliveries of raw materials a day. However, the drivers had taken to driving in "convoy pairs". This led to a bottleneck at unloading where the chemicals had to be tested and heated before they were pumped into the silos. The drivers then complained at having to wait! The impact on operations meant there was a resource demand to test and unload the raw materials. In the office this can be illustrated where documents (for example invoice approvals) are batched before being sent on to the payment step.

- Another example at a college where the enrolment process was reviewed, it took up to 2 weeks to get enrolled. The whole process from the student perspective was a series of queues to do a short activity spread over many offices at the college. There were no appointments, so students' arrival was unplanned and erratic.

- Process time variation: This can occur for number of reasons, typically where there is no standard work or there are equipment, machine, or IT reliability issues. In the college, as enrolment took place only once a year, the knowledge, skills, and people were lost year to year, so it required a significant effort to re-train every September.

- High utilisation leads to longer queues: As 100% utilisation is approached, the queue will approach infinity. The optimum utilisation is 80%. This allows for some variation in arrival and some process variation but also minimises the queue length. At the college the longest queues were at the activities that required all students to do – the initial data validation step where real demand was supplemented with "Failure Demand" (Freedom from Command and Control John Seddon) – students arriving with incorrect information, no certificates, proof of id, all requiring extra work to rectify failure demand.

Capture the wastes, issues, and opportunities for the future state

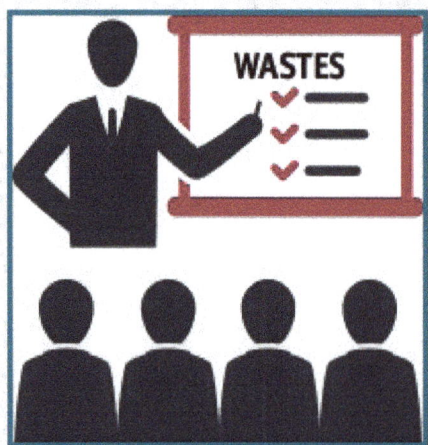

Collecting the wastes is also about gaining an understanding of the real issues in the process. Talking to the people who operate the process will reveal their issues and frustrations that occur daily. This also helps to answer the *what's in this for me* question as these frustrations will be addressed later in the action plan and the future state. These are all part of the waste capture activity as in the end they will impact the customer.

Once discussions start people will talk about the process as well as the data. They will raise complaints and issues or come up with ideas for improvement. These are all invaluable and need to be captured on an issues sheet – just on a flip chart is fine. They form the basis of getting engagement with people and answering the WIFM question – *what's in this for me*? These captured issues need to progress to help inform the future state as well as form part of the 3 Cs (concern-cause-countermeasure) first level problem solving we will discuss in step 5. Resolving these issues and reducing the overload or rework for people is part of the engagement process as we are making their work easier.

Issues are often hidden from clear view for example, a call centre, everyone is busy but what are they doing – it could be rework, complaints or perhaps just passing a customer from one person to the next. Business processes have typically not been improved in the same way as manufacturing so there is far more opportunity for improvement. However, discovery is harder as the process is hidden underneath the fog of day-to-day activity.

Examples of types of Data to Collect				
	Customer measure	**Customer measure**	**Input measure**	**Input measure**
Finance processes				
Accounts Payable	Days to pay supplier	Right first time payment	% Right first time Purchase orders	Input errors
Period close	Time to close accounts	Right first time	Number of plugs	Data received on time and accurate
HR processes				
Recruitment	Time to recruit from vacancy	Retention and promotions of recruits	Number of applicants	% Success from each recruitment stage
Leaving	Time to complete process	Right first time for pension, tax etc	% turnover rate	% Exit interviews conducted
Design services				
New business acquisition	Time to reach a specific stage	Overall end to end process time	Number of rework loops	Data received on time and accurate
Creation of an approved drawing	Time to reach a specific stage	Resource spend profile per stage	Rework loops	% Right first time

Example developed for one of the author's workshops

The table above provides several different examples of value driven measures as well as identifying enabling input measures. Although the table is not comprehensive it should provide enough breadth for the team to generate their own set of value driven metrics for the process being improved. The metrics need to enable customer value as well as align to the business objectives for the process improvement.

The data information is straightforward but collecting it may be difficult. Take care to explain what and why you are asking for this information. Quite often existing information and mind-sets are not aligned with process thinking. So, using the table above will help to open the door to a value driven set of metrics. It is important to maintain the focus and capture the reality of the process. How you present yourself and the questions you ask may drive the wrong answer. People get concerned if it looks like a time and motion study or they feel threatened or accused by the questions!

Tasks to complete:

Data Collection:

1. Use the data capture form to collect process data

2. Split into groups, split the process, work in parallel and then review in a plenary session to check data and engage the whole group

3. Go see - walk the process and talk to process users/subject matter experts/KPIs

4. Capture any relevant process data: -

   - Elapsed time, resource time and any variations
   - Data and information on problems / feelings
   - Capture decision points
   - Standards and evaluation criteria
   - Process Problems and Issues

5. You do not have to be 100% accurate to get information to be able to map the process, 80% is fine first time around - formal data collection may not exist, so fast vs perfect applies to get things moving.

Outputs from this step:

1. Completed data collection form (start to end of the process)

2. Problems and issues captured on flip chart List

3. Data reviewed together as team

		Data Collection for Business Process Improvement							
No	Date	Task	Who	Start time	End time	Time taken mins	Elapsed time (Days)	Standards	Notes
1									
2									
3									
4									
5									
6									
7									
8									
9									
10									

Step 4 Create a current state map

Creating a business process map with the team

After collecting the data, we are now ready to create the current state map. For those of you who have worked in manufacturing, it's the equivalent of value stream mapping in manufacturing – end to end process analysis. The only difference is that we use a different tool, flow chart mapping or swim lane as it's known in IT analysis.

The purpose of current state mapping is to understand the reality of what happens today. This may sound quite basic, but I can guarantee It will be different from any current record process. Things change quickly in business and if the process is over 12 months old it's highly likely to have changed. People may have moved on or joined, IT systems may have been updated, customer needs and supplier inputs may have altered, and regulations may have changed.

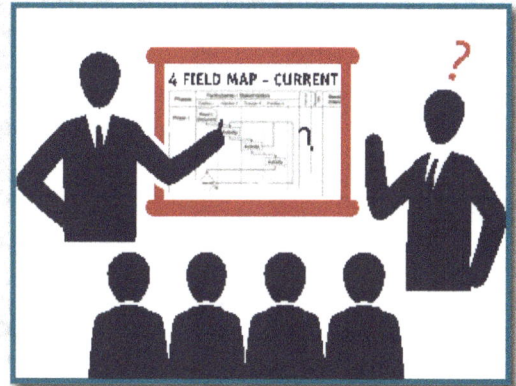

Engagement and consensus are the basis for improvement, so we need to create a single shared agreed view of the process. People / functions have different perspectives and leaders who are not close to the process may have a different view on how it works. IT interfaces and links need to be understood. Sometimes IT is used to speed up the process without considering the root causes of delays and errors. If standards exist, they should be used to check compliance and note any deviations.

If your process is large – multi-site/regional or global, you may need to create a bigger high-level picture of the process to enable it to be partitioned into manageable chunks for review. This is simply a block diagram covering the entire breadth of the process.

Create a high-level block diagram for multi-site, regional or global processes.

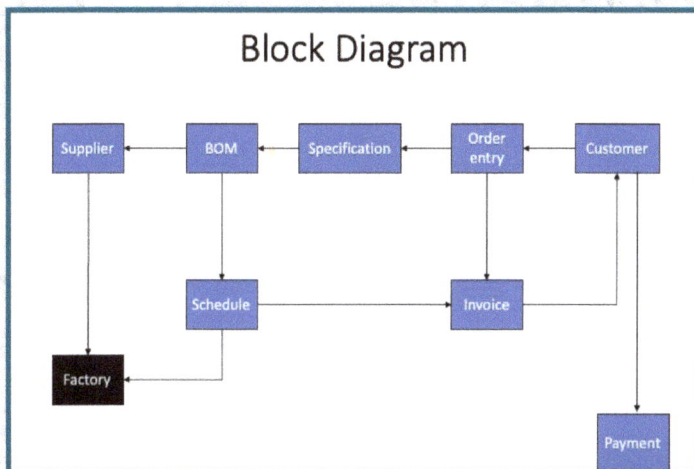

Block Diagram

Supplier → BOM → Specification → Order entry → Customer

Schedule → Invoice

Factory

Payment

A high-level block diagram helps visualise complex processes and can support the scoping process by visualising the key sub-processes. A good start point for the improvement workshop. A reference tool to keep on the wall. A check point for the workshop process Good for communication and engagement

The tool used for mapping a business process is called 4 field mapping. (Dimancescu and Dwenger World Class Product Development 1996). The first step of mapping a business process is to identify the process participants by function across the top in each of the separate columns. Remember, people change over time, but the function will remain the same, so we need to identify the function rather than the person on the map. There are up to 10 columns which naturally limits the number of functions that can be involved. If you have identified more than 10 functions, then it is likely the scope will need to be reviewed to break down the process into smaller pieces to review. These "function" columns can help identify who needs to be involved in the workshop – the "subject matter experts" of the process. The other option is to prioritise the functions most involved in the process and only include those.

Go-see the process as you map to capture reality

As with the data collection, go see the process and collect the data, information, issues, and wastes. This is an eye-opening activity especially for leaders who have previously managed at arm's length or more typically these days at the end of an email.

As part of the mapping, take time to "Go see" the actual process. Capture information and data through talking to process stakeholders. The process map needs to be based on reality and NOT "should be" status.

Example of a 4 Field map current state of the accounts payable process

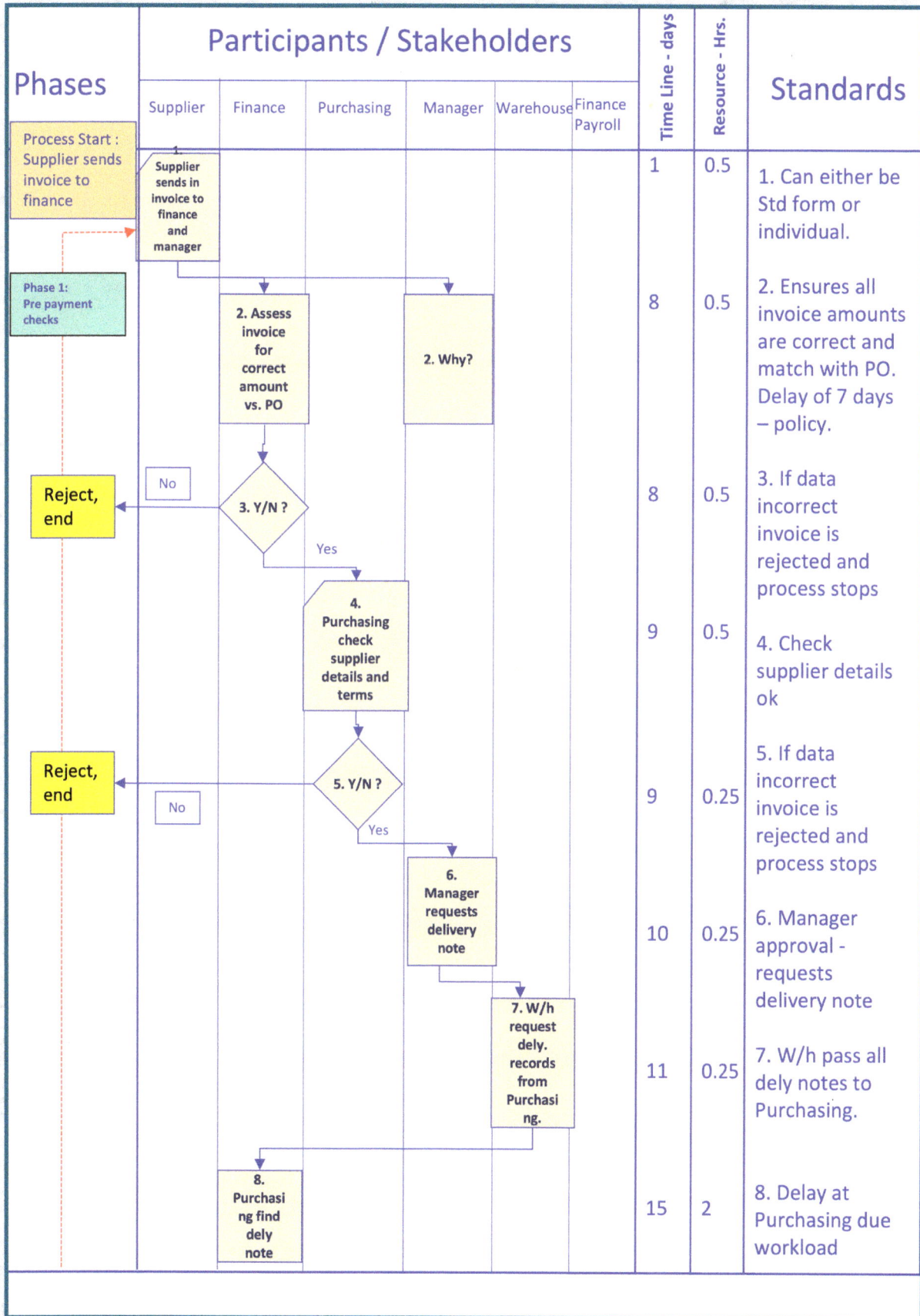

Phases	Participants / Stakeholders						Time Line - days	Resource - Hrs.	Standards
	Supplier	Finance	Purchasing	Manager	Warehouse	Finance Payroll			
Process Start : Supplier sends invoice to finance	1. Supplier sends in invoice to finance and manager						1	0.5	1. Can either be Std form or individual.
Phase 1: Pre payment checks		2. Assess invoice for correct amount vs. PO	2. Why?				8	0.5	2. Ensures all invoice amounts are correct and match with PO. Delay of 7 days – policy.
Reject, end		3. Y/N ? No					8	0.5	3. If data incorrect invoice is rejected and process stops
		Yes	4. Purchasing check supplier details and terms				9	0.5	4. Check supplier details ok
Reject, end			5. Y/N ? No				9	0.25	5. If data incorrect invoice is rejected and process stops
			Yes	6. Manager requests delivery note			10	0.25	6. Manager approval - requests delivery note
					7. W/h request dely. records from Purchasing.		11	0.25	7. W/h pass all dely notes to Purchasing.
		8. Purchasing find dely note					15	2	8. Delay at Purchasing due workload

Example from one of the author's process improvement workshops

The next step of mapping a business process current state is to understand the main phases of the process. Phases can be described as "chapters' of the process which are punctuated by key decisions. These phases are noted on left hand column of the process map. It helps orientate the reader by providing a higher-level structure for the process.

After the phases have been identified, the next step is creating the process map. Four simple icons are used:

A square to represent an activity

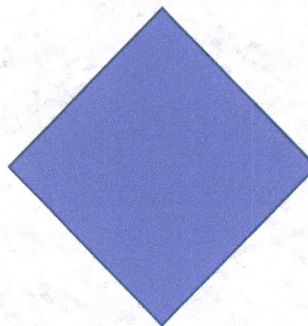

A diamond to represent a decision (Yes/No)

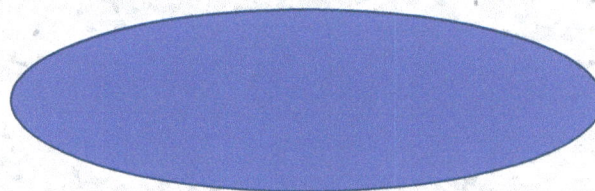

An oval to represent a meeting

A square with corner missing to represent a document (data or analysis – more than just communications).

Arrows are used to define the process flow vertically from top to bottom. A simple process map is shown below:

Process maps need to be clear follow a logic

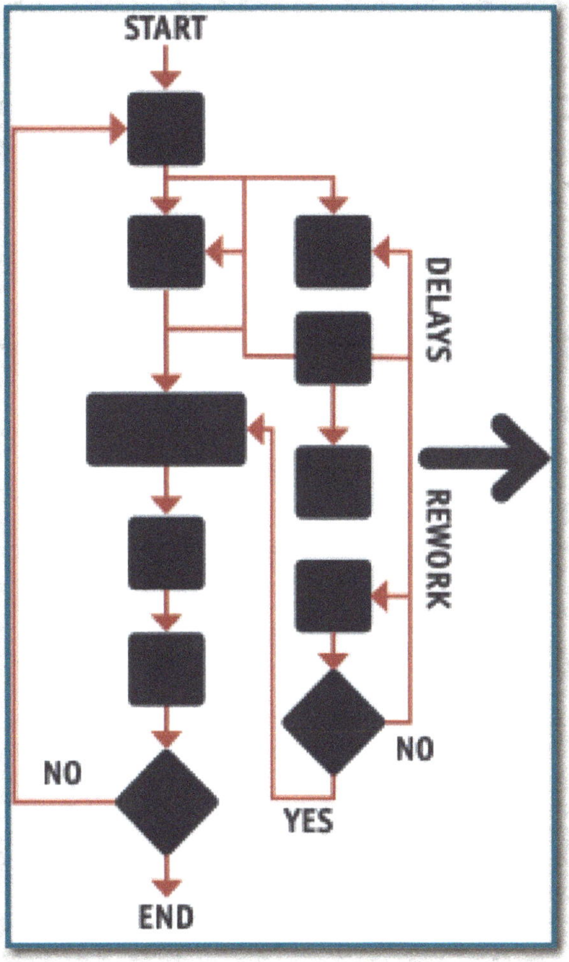

- In time order, sequentially
- Indicate activities in parallel next to each other, in sequence vertically linked
- Describe all steps in the process even if they do not make sense
- Take care to use the right icons
- Use pencil or post-it's to make changes easy

Check IT interfaces as you map the process. If it goes into an IT system you can treat it as a "black box" or as a step where the arrow leaves the process and comes back in again later in the process.

It's also important to understand if there are any system workflows that need mapping. IT is a key part of today's processes and cannot be ignored. Workflows are often put in place to accelerate processes by making communications electronic, however the potential root causes of behaviour are not addressed leading to delays which are inevitably embedded into the system.

If you want to dive into a "black box" you need to revise the scope to include this extension to the workshop

The process map is rarely created right first time as its difficult to map a process from scratch, so it's important to use post-its or pencil so that changes can be made easily. People have different views of a process, and these must be reconciled to one agreed version of the truth.

Once the map is complete, work though the process and add the lead time and resources time in the 2 columns to the right of the process map. For the lead time, it starts on day 1 and is typically measured in days. It is calculated cumulatively so that you can see delays and see how long each process step takes to complete. The resources are measured in hours – typically it's less than 1 hour so we see 0.5 or even 0.25 hrs for a task. Once complete the comparison between the two times provides an indication of the value added to non-value-added ratio.

A lead time and resources captured table

LEAD TIME (DAYS)	RESOURCES (HRS)	NOTES
0	2	1 Person for 2hrs
3	4	2 People for 2hrs each
7	8	8 People for 1hr
10	0.5	1 Person for 1/2hr
12	1.5	1 Person for 1.5hrs
17	0.25	1 Person for 1/4hr
49 Days	16.25hrs	

In this example the value added to non-value-added ratio is approximately 4% (2/49). This assumes all the work completed is value added. In business process we typically see figures of around 5% for the first cycle of improvement.

After the times, complete the standards column. This should be the criteria that apply to each step of the process. Do not be surprised if this information is missing, especially for a process that is being reviewed for the first time.

As with the data collection step, you will also receive comments and feedback about the process. It's important to continue to record these issues and wastes for resolution in the future state or in the action plan.

Finally consider an additional column – "RACI" This stands for:

R – responsible for doing the task, can be 1 or more people

A – accountable, the one person who is answerable for the task

C – consult, the person or people who are asked for their input before the task is done

I – inform, the person or people who are told after the task – be careful as some leaders whilst being informed think they are being consulted!

Tasks

- Create a current state process map
- Add data, lead time, resources, and standards to the map
- Capture the issues (both anecdotal) and factual that impact the process
- Calculate process analytics

Outputs

- Completed process map
- Process analytics (Lead time, value added time, non-value added time notional value %).

Step 5 Identify the wastes

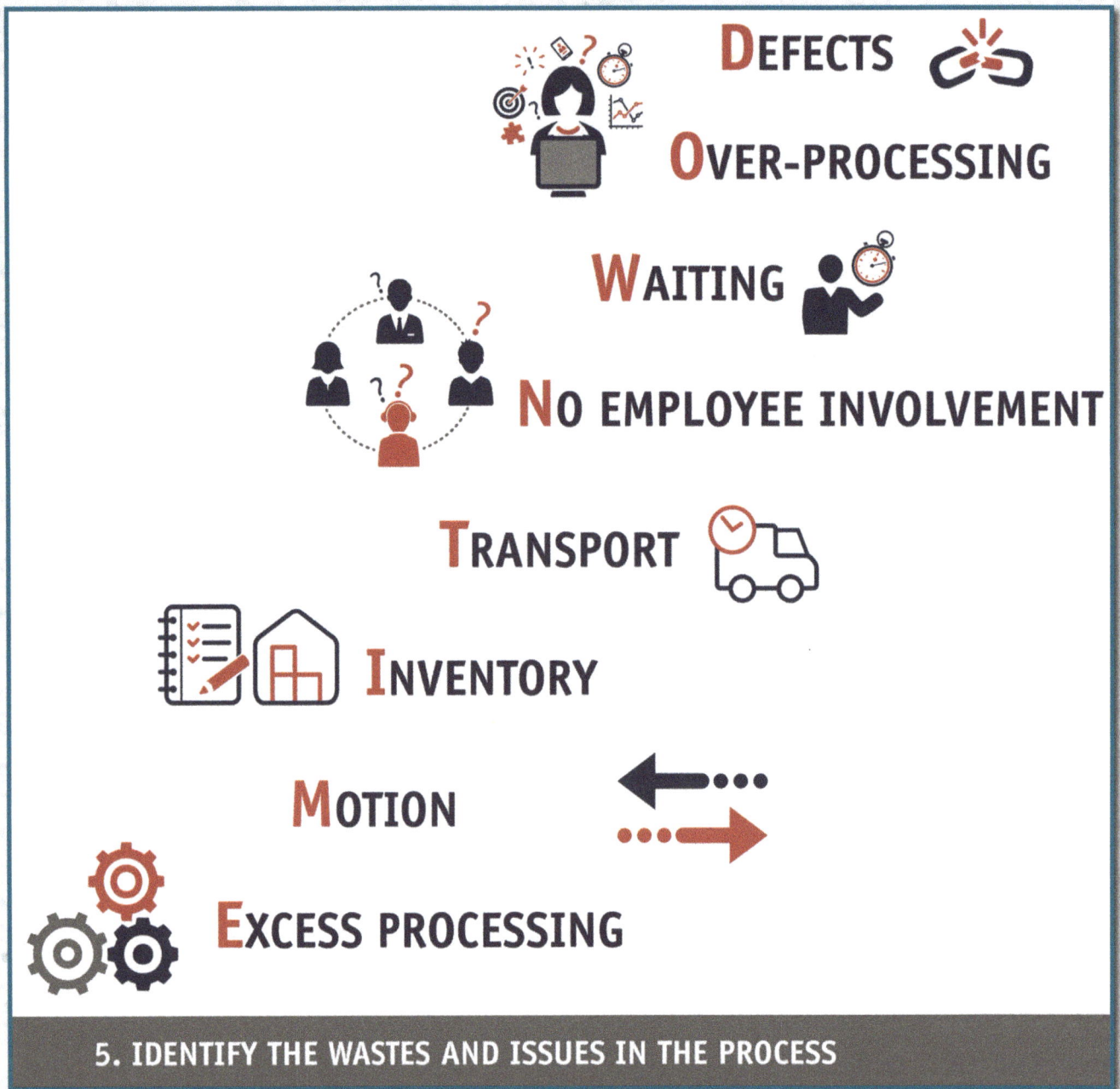

5. IDENTIFY THE WASTES AND ISSUES IN THE PROCESS

Once the current state map has been created and in addition to the issues and opportunities already identified, the process must be formally reviewed for wastes and issues. In this step we need to Understand value added and non-value-added activities in the process, identify wastes and process flow problems and additionally understand any monetary losses.

The classic 8 wastes adapted from the original 7 manufacturing wastes (Taiichi Ohno) are used to help us understand the process issues:

These wastes were originally developed through manufacturing and although the principles apply in business process it is useful to show how these wastes apply in the office.

The 8 Wastes applied to the factory office

Waste	Description	Example
Defects	An activity, service or information that is not right first time	Incorrect information Missing information Data entry errors Lost information
Over-Production	Producing more than is needed, producing faster than needed, duplication of process or effort	Emails to everyone Producing reports no-one reads Entering the same data on multiple forms/screens
Waiting	Delays caused by unsynchronised activities	Waiting for approvals Waiting for people – e.g., meetings Waiting for a response Waiting for information
No Employee involvement	Not using the skills and capabilities of employees	No involvement systems and structure No leadership skills supporting involvement No leadership coaching No training and development
Transport	Excessive movement of goods or information	Complicated process Excessive hand-offs Complicated and long supply chains Excessive approvals
Inventory	Unnecessary stock, materials, or data	Obsolete files and equipment Lack of memory space caused by excessive storage Excessive office supplies Printing too many documents
Motion	Excessive workplace motion	Searching for files Multiple systems required to do an activity New IT sitting on top of middleware to connect to legacy systems Office set up by function not by process
Excess Processing	Additional activity that creates no value to the process or service	Multiple approvals required Re-entering data Expediting reports/approvals Redundant steps in the process

We also need to understand the definition of value added and non-value added:

Value Added Criteria for each step:

- Customers cares about it
- Changes the fit form or function – moves process forward
- it's right first time

Non-value added:

- NVA - Wasteful activities that do not deliver value

Another way to describe the issues found in a business process are the 3Ms:

Muda Muri and Mura (Taiichi Ohno)

Muda: Stands for waste and is best described by "DOWNTIME" detailed on the previous diagram.

Mura: Stands for un-evenness Inconsistent workload. Can often be eliminated by leaders through level scheduling and careful attention to the pace of work

Muri: Stands for over-burden Requiring people or machines to operate at a higher pace, with more effort and for a longer time than appropriate / respectful level allows (target utilization @ 85%).

Bicheno 2016 suggests that the best sequence for improvement is Muri, Mura and then Muda, so find out what is impacting the people and machines first, level flow and demand and then get after the wastes.

From the current state map identify what are value added and non-value-added activities and using these definitions, the key issues and wastes are identified on the process map using simple green and red ticks for value add and non-value add.

This step is about understanding what is wrong with the process and what needs to be improved. The more issues and wastes we find the better it is. Do not worry if items are repeated, it just means they happen a lot and its more evidence that there is a problem. You will be able to pick the most relevant issues to resolve more easily

1. Mark the Current State Map with Identified NVA / VA on each process step
2. Get team to write up 8 wastes titles
3. Brainstorm all the wastes for this process
4. Categorise waste in their process under the title headings
5. Identify what needs to be prioritized and eliminated from the future state process

Process wastes also need to be identified - Non sequential process, where the process does not follow logic and "goes all over the place", serial activities where activities follow each other and are dependent on the previous step to be completed, delays of time caused by the process or service level agreements. Rework loops which are rather like snakes and ladders – you think you have finished a step only to have to go back to the start again. Waste can also exist within the shape of the process – it does not flow logically or clearly. All these factors impact the lead time – making it longer.

Identify the monetary losses related to this process. It's important to consider both tangible and intangible losses. Operational or intangible wastes are the ones that are surfaced first with Lean but yield little financial impact at the start. Quite often the intangible waste are the frustrations of the process so solving these answers the WIFM question (*what's in it for me?*) and generates engagement for the change process.

Highlight these key issues and wastes as starbursts on the process map. This provides a visual reference and reminder of the main issues and how and when they occur in the process.

Take the major wastes off the "Current state" Map and prioritise them onto 3C's chart

The 3 C's Table: Concern-Cause-Countermeasure

WASTE ANALYSIS – 3C TABLE

CONCERN	CAUSE		COUNTERMEASURE	
	PROCESS	BEHAVIOUR	PROCESS	BEHAVIOUR
1..........	....		....	
2........		....	....	....
3........	....	....	....	....

> Introducing a 3C table gets the team to dive deeper into the issue to get closer to the root cause. Identifying the correct root cause enables effective countermeasures to be developed.

This is called a 3C table:

- **C**oncern
- **C**ause
- **C**ountermeasures

It is the first level of basic problem solving. The concern is the main issue or waste. The cause is the first level of analysis – quite often sufficient if you are looking at a process for the first time, but don't be afraid to dive deeper and ask the 5 whys here to get to the root cause. The countermeasures are what you must do to make it right

Collect all the issues from the process, flip charts and post-its and enter them into the concern column. Any process wastes or issues are also noted in the concern column. This represents the perceived source of waste the next stage of process and behaviour analysis. Behaviours are a key root cause for business process, in fact most of the causes are behavioural. This is a systematic way to solve problems. It provides the foundation for the action plan at the end of the workshop. At this stage you can also group and prioritise the top 5 key items – use the affinity process.

Tasks:

1. Current State Map marked visually with Identified NVA / VA decision on each process step

2. Team to categorise waste in their process

3. Brainstorm all the wastes for this process under the title headings

4. To help identify what needs to be prioritized and eliminated from the future state process

Outputs:

- Visual process map showing the value and non – value steps

- Wastes categorised and prioritised

Step 6 Create the future state

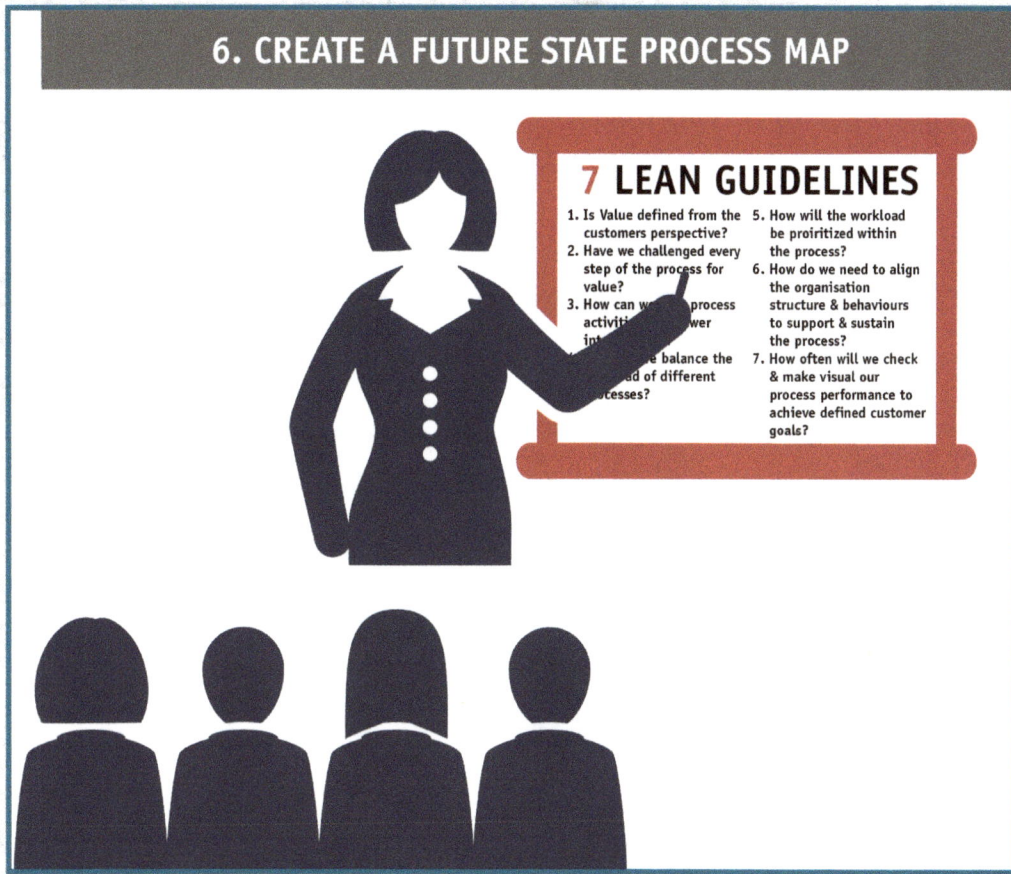

6. CREATE A FUTURE STATE PROCESS MAP

7 LEAN GUIDELINES

1. Is Value defined from the customers perspective?
2. Have we challenged every step of the process for value?
3. How can we [...] process activiti[...] [...]wer int[...]
[...] balance the [...]d of different [...]cesses?

5. How will the workload be proiritized within the process?
6. How do we need to align the organisation structure & behaviours to support & sustain the process?
7. How often will we check & make visual our process performance to achieve defined customer goals?

To create the future state, we must first reference the issues and wastes that have been identified. For each issue or group of issues (one theme) identify the root cause of the problem using either causality, 5 whys or a simple fishbones analysis. Work through each line across – from cause to countermeasure defining process and behaviour issues as required. Once completed move to the next column to identify the countermeasures.

The **causes** and **countermeasure**s are again split into to two areas – process and behaviour.

Process concerns are direct concerns surrounding the current structure of the process.

Behaviour concerns are a large factor in the causes of wastes compared to process work design "I don't want to, I don't have to, I did not know etc" are often statements heard when analysing business processes.

Getting to the root cause will ensure the right countermeasures are selected. Often the surface waste is addressed, and this does not solve the problem. It's important to recognise that its difficult to change behaviours as they are close to an individual's core values so you may need several actions to make it happen.

The next step is creating the future state process map. Start with the existing current state and review the previously added green and red ticks.

The picture below shows a completed process map with green ticks for the value added and red crosses for the non-value-added steps. The visual representation provides the challenge that the future state should simply be just the green ticks.

A current state business process map with the value added and non-value added steps visualised.

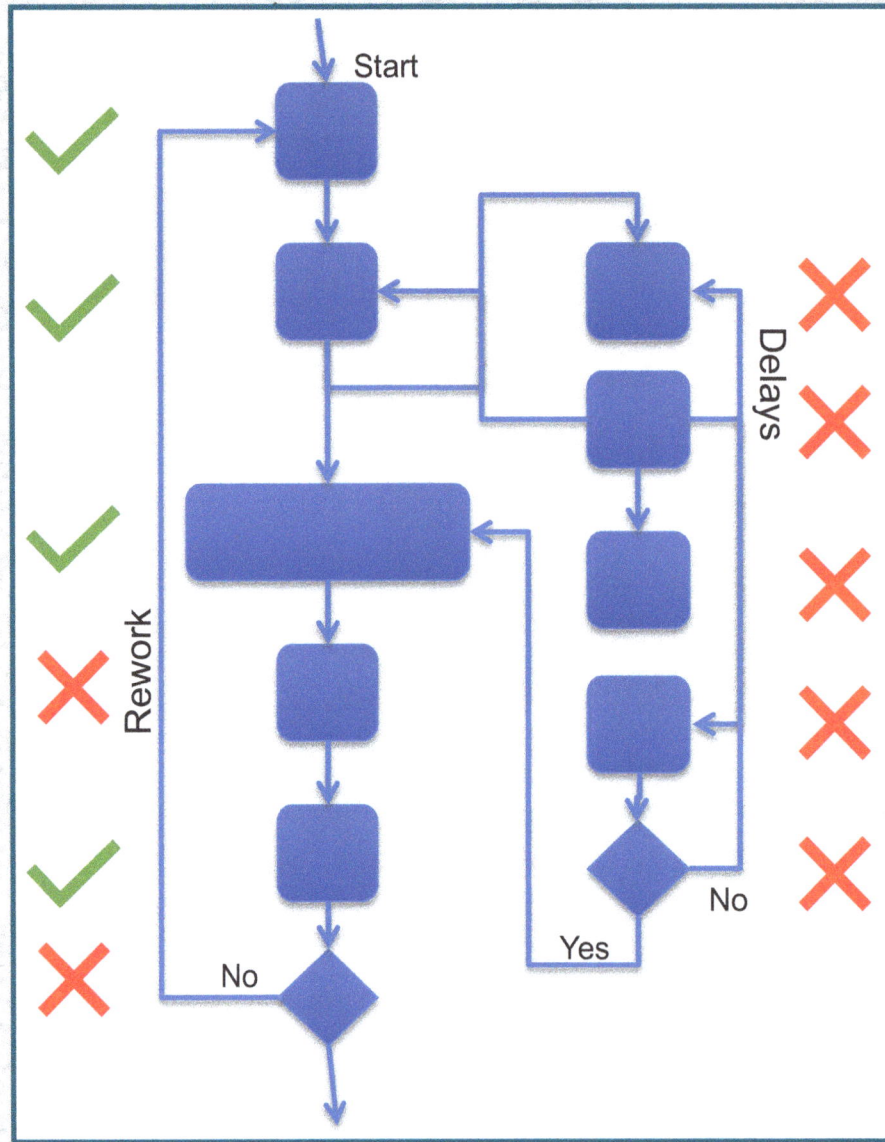

Once the current state has been reviewed, use the 7 Lean guidelines, and see how they apply to the process.

Use the 7 Lean guidelines to help shape the future state

Guideline	Description
1. Is value defined from the customers perspective?	Identify the customers: "Who needs the output of the process?" Ask "what do they value?" Stakeholders have a vested interest in the process and need to be consulted on their value
2. Have we challenged every step of the process for value?	The 3 rules for value: 1. Customers care about it 2. Changes the fit, form or function – moves process forward 3. Its right first time
3. How can we flow process activities with fewer interruptions?	Consider the shape of the process. Introduce parallel activities where possible. Standardise activities, introduce a RACI matrix, visualise the process. Eliminate any turn-backs or rework and avoid a snakes and ladders operations by making objectives clear at the start.
4. How can the workload be balanced?	Prioritise the work, use Hejunka load levelling
5. How will it be prioritised?	Focus on the customer needs and values and align the work. Use techniques like SCRUM and SPRINT.
6. How do we need to align the organisation structure and behaviours to support and sustain the process?	Build on RACI Set up cross functional process teams, visualise the process and/or co-locate.)
7. How often will we check and make visual our process performance to achieve defined customer goals?	Use visual monitoring systems so status is clear and aligned to demand. Leadership standard work should validate performance

Key here are:

RACI: Responsibility matrix: Responsible, Accountable, Consult, Inform

SCRUM: A method of prioritising managing complex activities

SPRINT: A method of delivering complex sets of activities to ensure customer value.

In addition to the 7 Lean guidelines, follow up the lessons from Kingman equation in step 3:

- Stay away from high utilisation – trade off good usage of the process step with low lead time
- Reduce variation: This will allow a lower stock level and reduce peak resource demand
- If you have high variability lower utilisation
- If you have high utilisation lower variability

Create a future state process map, to make a step change to process performance and value delivery. Creating a good future state needs value, lead time, quality and right first time to be considered.

The next stage is to create the KPIs. To do this, review process value, understand the critical points/ outputs of the process and create KPIs to drive the right process behaviour. Ideally these KPIs should be enabling – i.e., be able to impact the future performance of the process and not reporting on what has happened already. Process controls also need to be considered to error proof and reveal problems straight away. These can be through visual or automated systems.

There are big positives and negatives for IT use in business process. Legacy systems and cost of change make IT challenging, and it seems there is always a newer better one around the corner. IT is not always thought of as an enabler to the process but as an entity itself which must be served. Where it works, it is focussed on customer needs and values most of all.

Having considered all 7 Lean guidelines above it is now time to create the future state process map. Using post-its and a blank 4 Field map create a future state. As each step is created ask again – do we need to do this? Can we do this quicker or better? As the discussion progresses with the team, further ideas develop and can be triggered by other discussions to reduce lead time. Think about eliminating steps, introducing effective launch communication meetings to ensure sharing and consistency, parallel activities, removing rework through standards and ensuring key decisions are not left to the end of the process. It's important to keep an eye for the future, what is the ideal state? – the long-term vision. This will help to stretch the thinking and help break the actions down into manageable chunks

The future state should also be used to compress lead time, address problems / waste through the process shape (parallel working, simple process, no rework, early aligned decisions, effective communication events) so that every opportunity is taken to improve the process.

The transition between current and future state should be a visual step change

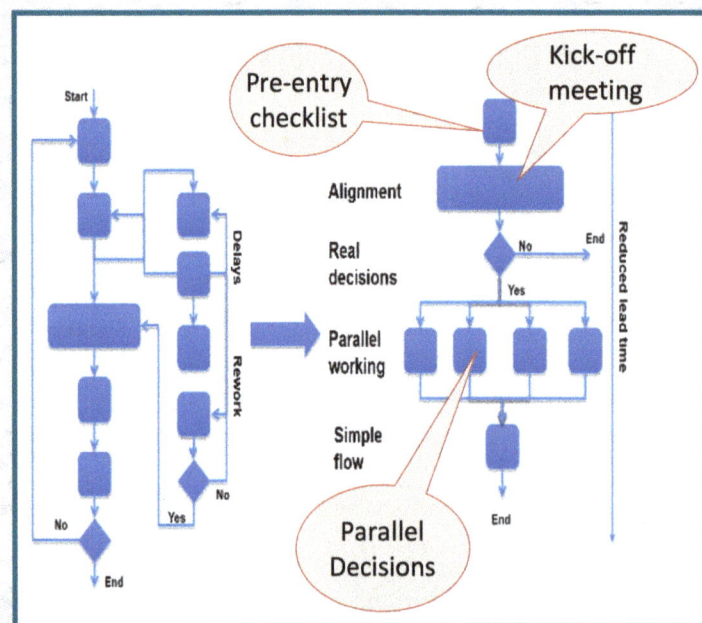

The future state on the right-hand side demonstrates several key enablers to flow:

At the start of the process is a pre-entry checklist to make sure all information is available before the start of the process and that any new work is aligned to the process and can be progressed without chasing. The first activity is a kick-off meeting to ensure all participants are aligned and know the objectives. Any early objections or rejections need to be surfaced at this meeting to ensure that time and effort is not wasted subsequently – this is visualised through the early go/no-go gate decision. Once into the meat of the process, parallel working of activities is scheduled to compress the lead time. Although this requires more management, namely in the form of a process manager supported by visualisation, it will save work in the long term. Finally, the process should be pleasing to the eye and provide a clear, simple, logical process flow

Tasks

- Create a future state map, use this to address the issues identified from the current state and make a step change in the process
- Create a comparison table of lead time and resources between the current state and the future state so that the benefits are clear

Outputs

- Future state process map
- Reduced lead time, improved quality, and effective use of resources
- Streamlined process fit for purpose

Step 7 Action and Communications planning

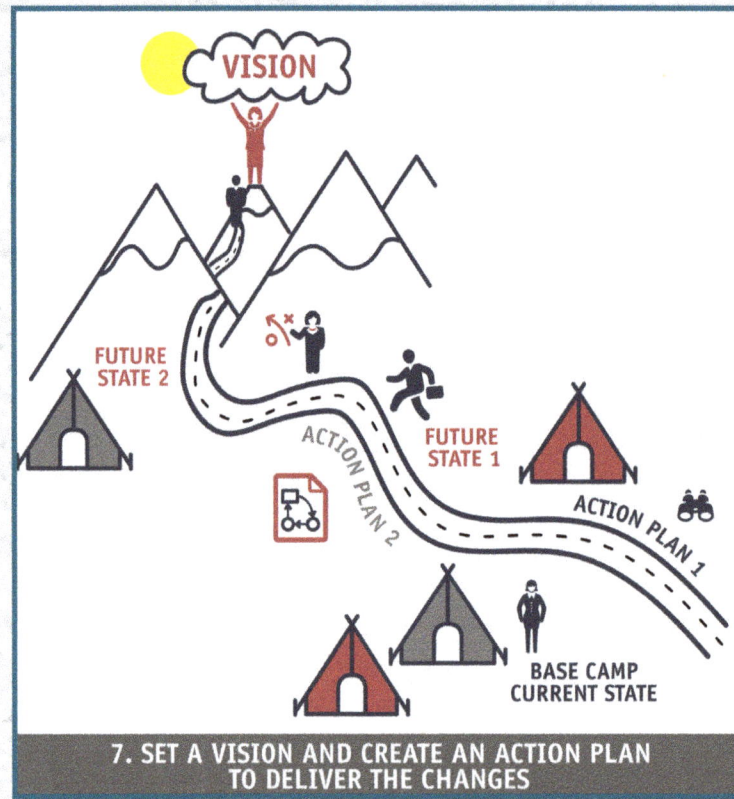

7. SET A VISION AND CREATE AN ACTION PLAN TO DELIVER THE CHANGES

The action plan should be treated as a journey up a mountain, with camps set up to regularly review progress, check weather and conditions, and change direction or amend the plan as necessary – just like you would if you were climbing a mountain for real.

There are 4 key elements in this step:

1. Create an action plan that will deliver the future state process
2. Develop a communication plan to share information
3. Create Leaders' Standard Work to sustain the gains made through the improvement activity
4. Create a culture of continuous improvement via employee engagement and leadership designed to do so

The action plan needs to deliver the future state, resolve the issues, and move to the vision for the process within the business

The action plan defines the activities required to deploy the future state, it also defines the actions to resolve the issues and eliminate the wastes. It should consider the steps towards the vison for the organisation and this process. The plan should form the base camp and stages to the top of the mountain. The plan needs to be developed using the team and the people who are going to do the work. Often people just focus on (what) actions and not when and who so it's important to get ownership for actions, targets, and due date. The due dates should be structured to enable a rapid deployment. Typically, the first quick and easy actions have the biggest impact and motivate the team to do the rest.

The action and communications plan are created and owned by the team

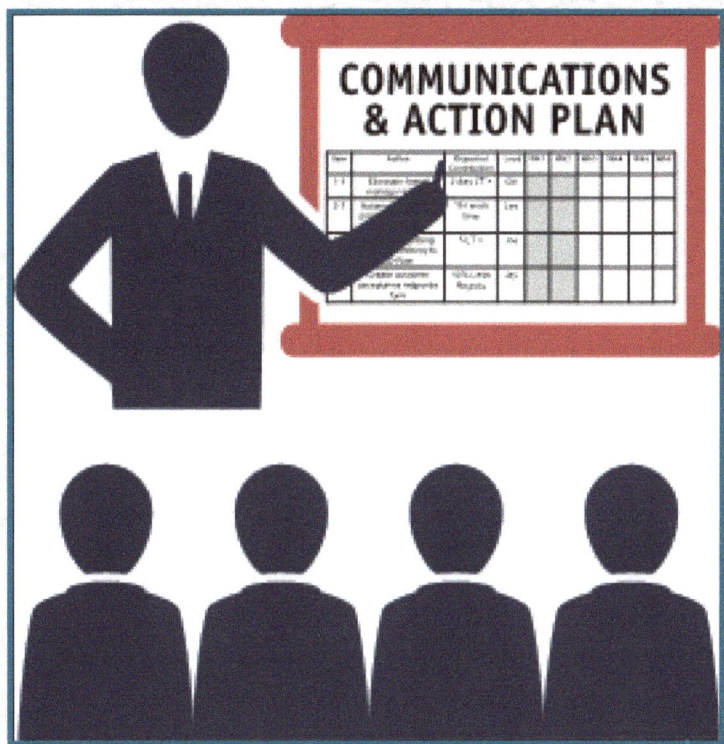

The workshop is the "fun" part, were discovery and understanding provide energy to the team. Now with the action plan starts the tough phase, agreeing what needs to change and delivering the plan.

To create the action plan, firstly list all the actions that develop from the counter measures from the 3 C table and include any other actions picked up in the workshop from your issues capture flip chart. The next step is the most important - Identify the person will be accountable for the action to be delivered in the room and ask them to determine further resources and a timeframe for completion – challenge their view if it appears excessive but remember the time for an action must be owned by the person doing the action. Ownership for actions is key, as without an owner the action will not get completed. The final step is to develop a visual Implementation plan for the improvement actions

The communications plan is easily overlooked, and the overall impact of the changes needed are not fully considered. The team has been working hard to develop an improved process from its own perspective, but others in the organization are probably not aware of what changes are being considered and may have some input to give of their own. Here it's important to use the team to determine the level of impact on the different groups of people. Identify the audiences, how they will be impacted, what they need to know and then design the content and medium to suit.

The communications will vary from a simple email or notice to full training session dependant on how much the changes impact people.

Both the action and communications plan need to be displayed visually and checked for implementation through leader standard work.

Action and communications plans are also tracking documents to ensure completion

Change Plan

No	What	Who	Impact	When							Status
1											
2											
3											
4											
5											
6											
7											
8											
9											
10											

Note that actions are limited to 10 – it's all too easy to generate a long list of actions that will seem daunting and not get implemented. It's far better to assess the actions of those that deliver a high impact and are easy to do. If the actions get completed quickly and deliver the desired improvements, it's time to move onto the next process.

Impact- Ease 2x2 matrix

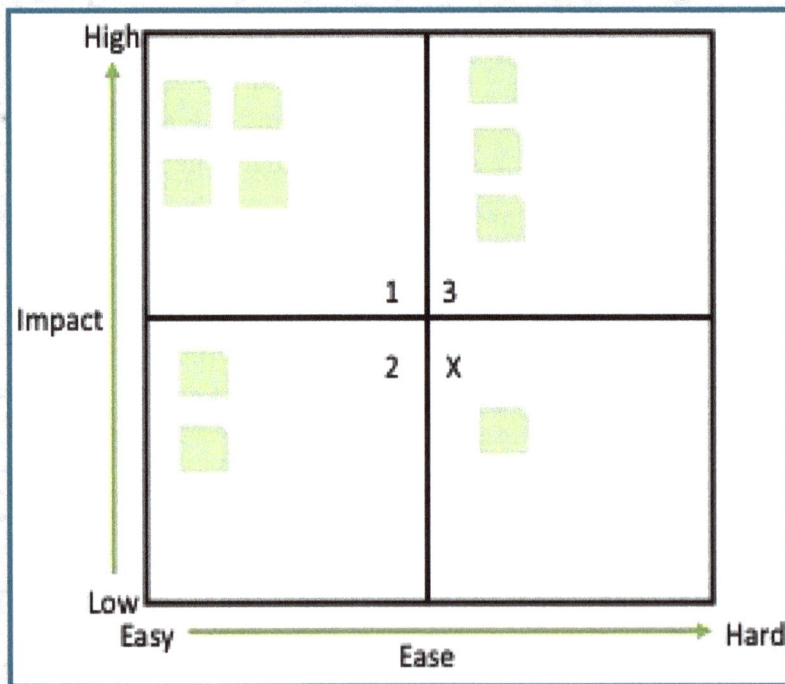

A 2x2 matrix is probably the quickest and easiest way to prioritise or classify actions. It is very inclusive and forms a good system to gain consensus.

Draw up the simple template on a flip chart. Get the team to write down the actions – one on each post-it. Then stick each action in the approximate box – work through data ideally, otherwise through the consensus of the team. The order of completion is 1-3, the easy/high impact actions first followed by the easy/low impact actions and then finally the high impact hard to do actions. The hard to do low impact actions should not be tackled.

The communication plan is similar in format to the action plan

Communication Plan

No	What is the change	Who will be impacted	Action	When						Status
1										
2										
3										
4										
5										
6										
7										
8										
9										
10										

Care needs to be taken to evaluate the impact of the change on the different teams and individuals. The action needs to be designed to address the personal impact of the change to the team and the person.

One of the biggest criticisms of Lean deployment is the lack of sustainment of implementation of the future state. The euphoria of the workshop and the motivation it creates can soon be lost with the day-to-day pressures of the day job. Unlike the factory, office processes continue when you are not there so the reward for improvement is sometimes a bigger in-tray!

The difficulties in sustaining change

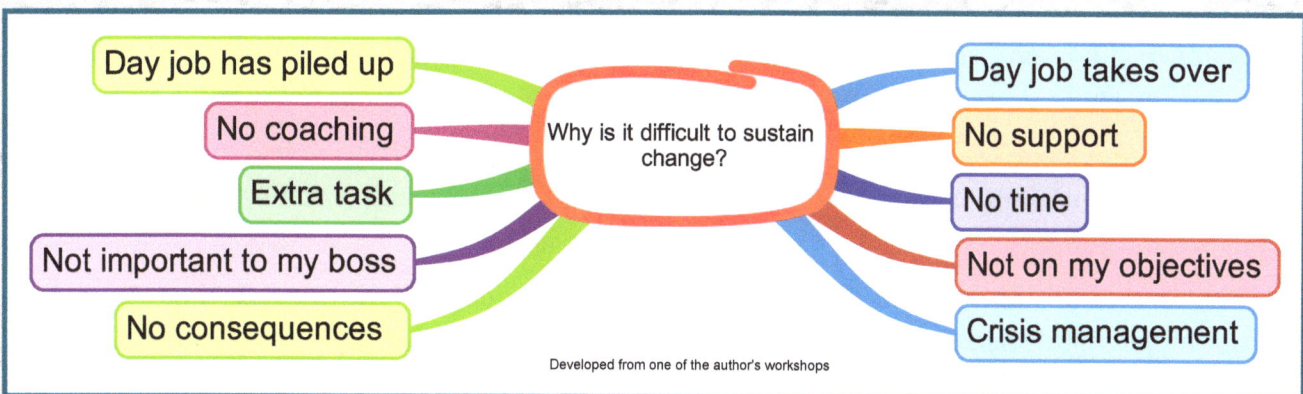

Why is it difficult to sustain change?

Day job has piled up — No coaching — Extra task — Not important to my boss — No consequences — Day job takes over — No support — No time — Not on my objectives — Crisis management

Developed from one of the author's workshops

There are many reasons why change fails. All the above seems to be common sense management. However, with the pressures of daily work it is all too easy to do the urgent and forget the important.

Countermeasures to the barriers to change

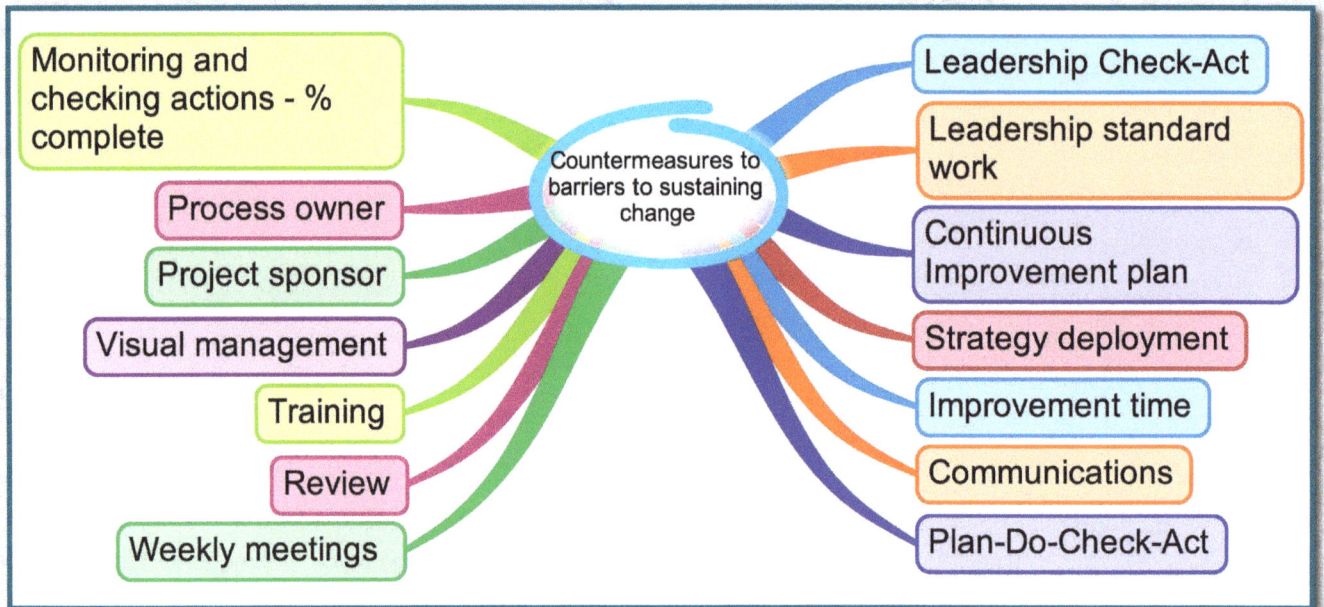

Developed from one of the author's workshops

Although there are a lot of barriers to change if we start thinking about the future before it arrives, it is possible to deploy many countermeasures to ensure success of the improvement activity. It starts with leader's support, their ownership, and Leaders'

Standard Work described below. Simple activities like tracking the progress of actions on a regular basis will motivate individuals to keep up with their own actions. Regular reviews keep the focus on the actions and weeds out actions that are more of a wish list.

Leaders' Standard Work is key to ensuring actions are implemented.

Everyone is watching the leader. They are watching the leader for their actions and clues to what they should do and what they don't need to do. The questions they ask and the checks the leader makes determines how the team responds and behaves. What's important to the leader soon becomes important to the team. That's why top-down support is key to Lean deployment. If the leader is checking and asking about the Lean actions, then Lean becomes important to the team.

Leaders' Standard Work is a systematic method of identifying the critical points of any process or operation, defining the questions to ask or parameters to challenge and coaching for improvement where there are gaps.

Leaders need to be engaged and develop their Leaders' Standard Work to check that actions are being completed, this needs to be visible to all so that there are clear expectations of performance and set into a routine so that it is completed to a pattern that ensures the momentum of the change is continued.

One of the ways of operating Leader's Standard Work is using Kamishibai cards. The original meaning is "paper drama", it is a form of storytelling that originated in Japanese Buddhist Temples in the 12th century, where monks used picture scrolls to convey stories with moral lessons. As part of the Toyota Production System, a Kamishibai board is used as a visual control for performing audits within a manufacturing process.

The cards detail the checks and frequency that the leader needs to do. They are displayed at the point of use and are visual in their nature – the status of the checks can easily be determined as can the follow up actions and their status.

Example Kamishibai Card:

Leaders Standard Work
Department
Name
Function:
Timing:
Daily Actions/Questions: 1. Attend morning meeting, review KPIs and actions 2. Resolve and health and safety concerns 3. Check 1 process in detail for performance 4. Coach 1 employee daily 5. Recognise 1 employee daily
Weekly Actions 1. Attend Tuesday supply chain review 2. Attend Wednesday management meeting 3. Collate weekly quality stats 4. Coach 1 problem solving activity 5. Highlight 3 improvement ideas

The style shown below is more popular with senior leaders, as their life is often run by a busy calendar. In the example the Leader's standard work has been incorporated into the leader's diary, so it forms the template of their work and is also visible to others.

Leadership Standard Work

Updated on Sept 24th, 2018

		MON	TUE	WED	THU	FRI	Comments
Daily	8:00 am		8:20AM - 8:30AM Tier 1 Meeting Production Dept 8:30AM - 8:45AM 5S Audit, Plant Tour	8:20AM - 8:30AM Tier 1 Meeting Quality Dept 8:30AM - 8:45AM 5S Audit, Plant Tour	8:20AM - 8:30AM Tier 1 Meeting Engineering & R&D 8:30AM - 8:45AM 5S Audit, Plant Tour	8:20AM - 8:30AM Tier 1 Meeting Purchase Dept 8:30AM - 8:45AM 5S Audit, Plant Tour	
	9:00 am	9:15 - 9:30AM Ops meeting 9:30AM - 12:00AM Weekly Sales Meeting in Milan Office	9:30 - 9:45 AM Ops meeting 9:45AM - 10:00AM Manager Talk, Production Dept	9:30 - 9:45 AM Ops meeting 9:45AM - 10:00AM Manager Talk, Quality Dept	9:30 - 9:45 AM Ops meeting 9:45AM - 10:00AM Manager Talk, R&D & R&D Dept	9:30 - 9:45 AM Ops meeting	
	10:00 am		10:00PM - 11:30PM Weekly Review Meeting	10:00AM - 10:15AM Manager Talk, HR	10:00AM - 10:15AM Manager Talk, Finance	10:00AM - 10:15AM Manager Talk, Purchase	
	11:00 am 12:00 pm						
	1:00 pm		1:00PM - 2:00PM Daily Production Meeting	1:00PM - 2:00PM Daily Production Meeting	1:00PM - 2:00PM Daily Production Meeting	1:00PM - 2:00PM Daily Production Meeting	
	2:00 pm	2:00PM - 3:00PM SH - DY	2:00PM - 2:30PM Plant Tour	2:00PM - 2:30PM Plant Tour	2:00PM - 2:30PM Plant Tour 15:00PM -16:00PM	2:00PM - 2:30PM Plant Tour	
	3:00 pm					3:00PM - 4:00PM	
	4:00 pm	4:00PM - 5:30PM Weekly Review			Extra Meeting - LEAN	Weekly Product Launch	
	5:00 pm		5:15PM - 5:30PM 5S Audit, Plant Tour	5:15PM - 5:30PM 5S Audit, Plant Tour	5:15PM - 5:30PM 5S Audit, Plant Tour	4:40PM - Leave for London	
	6:00 pm						

Daily Focus

MON	TUE	WED	THU	FRI
☑ Sales / ☐ R&D	☑ Sales / ☐ R&D	☑ Sales / ☐ R&D	☑ Sales / ☐ R&D	☐ Sales / ☐ R&D
☐ Production / ☐ Engineering	☐ Production / ☐ Engineering	☐ Production / ☐ Engineering	☐ Production / ☐ Engineering	☐ Production / ☐ Engineering
☑ Quality / ☐ Purchase	☑ Quality / ☐ Purchase	☑ Quality / ☐ Purchase	☑ Quality / ☐ Purchase	☑ Quality / ☑ Purchase
☐ Product Launch / ☐ Lean	☐ Product Launch / ☐ Lean	☐ Product Launch / ☐ Lean	☐ Product Launch / ☐ Lean	☐ Product Launch / ☐ Lean
☑ HS&E	☑ HS&E	☑ HS&E	☑ HS&E	☑ HS&E

Monthly
1. Management Meeting
2. SSC Meeting
3. Universal Holding Staff Meeting
4. Operational Result Meeting (TBD)
5. Global Market Meeting
6. Global Sales Meeting

Quarterly
1. Italy Leadership Meeting, organized by Italy Holding
2. Italy Commercial Managers Meeting

Annually
1. Employee Town Meeting (2 Times per Year)
2. Sales Meeting (2 Times per Year)
3. Budget Meeting
4. Capex Meeting
5. Strategy Meeting

Leader's standard work is not just for the top of the organisation. It is a layered system where every leader, manager and supervisor have their own set of checks, questions and coaching to perform. It's the responsibility of each leader to check that their subordinates are performing their Leader's standard work as well. You may ask, who checks the senior leaders? At that level it could be a peer review or someone impartial in the team – the continuous improvement leader for example.

> A continuous improvement culture can be created if employees can see a genuine path to improving their work and their place of work. The way all leaders are trained and developed is systematically geared to develop continuous improvement thinking and methodology. Leader's Standard is implemented to support the culture.

Rapid Mass Engagement and CI Leadership

A highly successful (see Shingo Prize winners in Europe 2010-17) approach to creating a continuous improvement culture is Devine's Rapid Mass Engagement process (Devine 2016). This method focuses on changing the culture of an organisation by setting and aligning the beliefs and values of the employees and leaders with the organisation and by creating 'employee pull for Lean' (Devine & Bicheno, 2019). It focuses on removing the negative filters that build up over time within organisations. Accountability is increased both for leaders and employees through a bespoke leadership system called the "Cathedral Model" see below. (Brophy 2012, Devine 2016)

Every year Frank Devine runs hundreds of workshops where employees describe how they see their leaders and their organisations (a key part of the Rapid Mass Engagement process which compliments the leadership approach outlined here). Employees hear their leaders describe what appears to be the same issues in very different ways depending on individual leaders' organisational and educational experiences and favoured models. This complexity is experienced by many employees not as evidence of sparkling intellectual diversity but rather as a lack of alignment and competence! The Cathedral/ Higher Purpose Model explained below reverses this process and delivers a few key skills well and often enough to move the culture forward. Use of the cathedral model in tandem with Leaders' Standard Work provides a system and structure to grow leadership skills, increase the accountability and make a positive step towards a sustainable Lean culture.

The model is illustrated here:

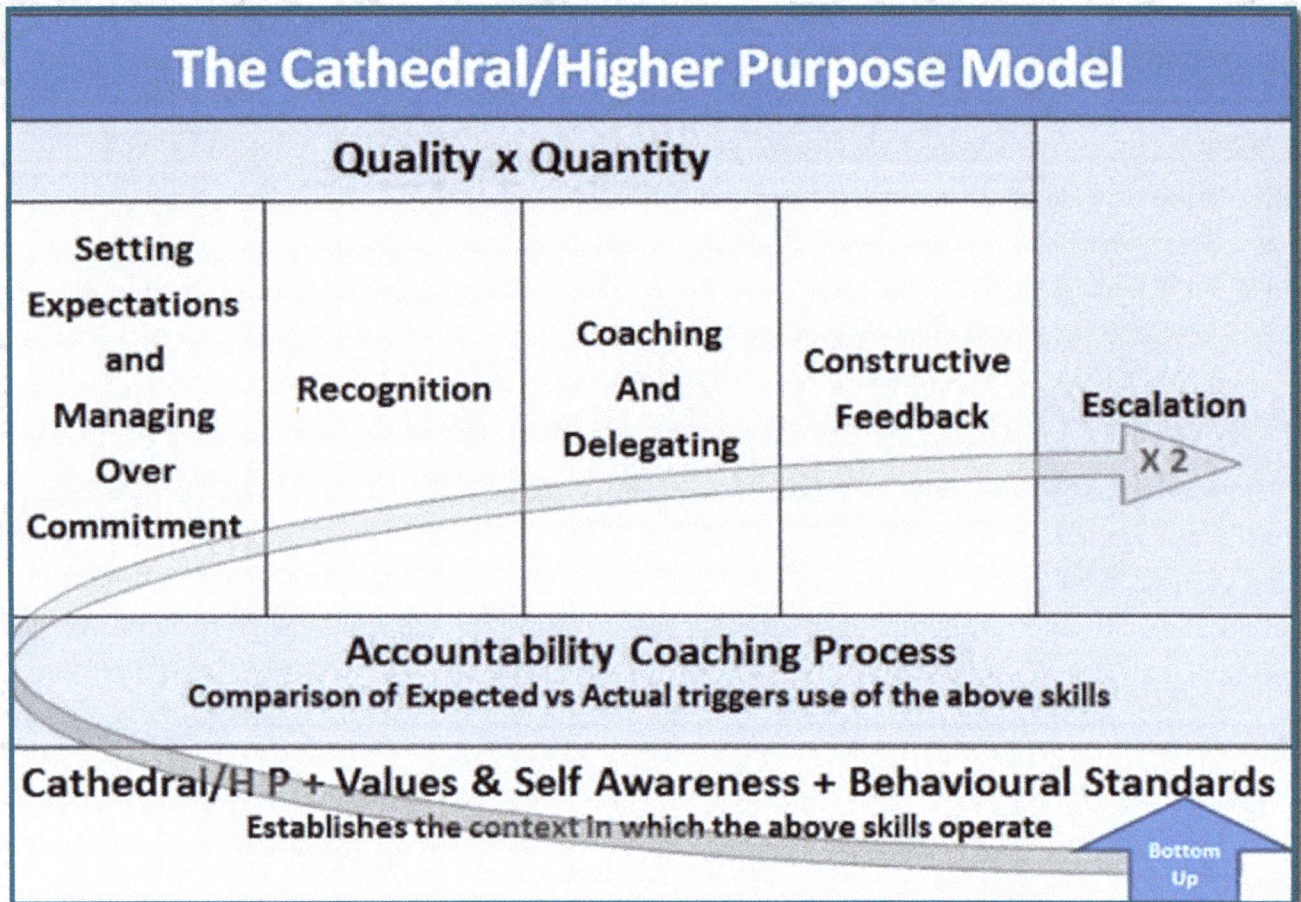

The Cathedral/Higher Purpose Model

Quality x Quantity				
Setting Expectations and Managing Over Commitment	Recognition	Coaching And Delegating	Constructive Feedback	Escalation X 2
Accountability Coaching Process Comparison of Expected vs Actual triggers use of the above skills				
Cathedral/H P + Values & Self Awareness + Behavioural Standards Establishes the context in which the above skills operate				Bottom Up

The name "Cathedral model" comes from the story of 2 brick builders who were asked the question – "what are you doing?". One answered laying bricks, the second answered building a Cathedral – the higher purpose. Many leaders see the logical significance of the second bricklayer's response, - that he sees the big picture and where his work fits within it. Unfortunately, many leaders miss the emotional aspect of his response, his pride in his work.

It starts with the foundations of behavioural standards. This is an agreement, not an imposition, of how people will behave on a day-to-day basis in a highly consistent way. A typical standard found is: "don't walk by" – if something is wrong or unsafe, stop and rectify or escalate to get something done. The next foundation stone is the daily accountability process which is a process for systematically sustaining both leaders' skills and all other standards in an organisation. This helps to get around the "I'm too busy" excuse and embeds the new culture through the introduction of a system to change behaviours.

The next step is the setting of expectations or objectives, making it clear what the standards area and what is acceptable and un-acceptable behaviour. The next 3 elements need to be implemented with a high quality and quantity to enable the leader to earn the right to move across the model from recognition to constructive feedback as the situation demands.

The arrow in the model has 2 meanings:

1. It demonstrates the sequential nature of the model:

    Progress starts with building a strong foundation of creating a sense of Cathedral, and sometimes a shared Higher Purpose, based on values and behavioural standards.

    It then adds brilliant basics skills all delivered at very high levels of quality and quantity.

    Finally, these are continuously improved by the application of the accountability coaching process. (Similar to "Check, Act" in PDCA)

2. It is not enough to deliver individual skills in isolation to the quality recommended. The model is a system which starts with the foundation steps of leadership values and accountability. It then moves from left to right. Leaders "earn the right" to move rightwards in the model i.e., become more assertive and directional where appropriate.

    Everyone will have their natural style – recognition/constructive feedback and many people will also defer from moving to the right to use constructive feedback and consequences. However, moving to the right of the model has a much larger impact on the behaviour of people than staying on the left, hence the direction and position of the arrow.

A summary of key outputs from the different sections of this dynamic system of leadership follows:

Setting expectations:

The purpose of this question is to answer the question "I know what is expected of me at work". Setting expectations is done by mutually agreeing what we expect from each other, this reinforces values around respect, teamwork, and mutuality inherent in the foundation level discussed above.

Managing over commitment:

Interviewed for this book Devine explained:

"We do this by establishing mutual expectations with both the commitment-seeker and the commitment-giver so that the cumulative impact of employees' workload is calculated, and appropriate adjustments made. By so doing we not only de-risk against random (and therefore, potentially catastrophic) failure but protect the moral basis on which the new culture sits, a key aspect of a sustained high-performance culture."

Recognition:

In the Cathedral/Higher Purpose Model recognition is given because it is the right thing to do not because we want something in return; it has a values-based purpose. Devine deliberately contrasts this unconditional recognition with the conditional approaches to recognition so common in conventional approaches.

Coaching and delegating:

Devine deliberately fuses learning from CI and more conventional approaches to coaching.

The aim is to:

- Add rigour to coaching especially re understanding data and challenging assumptions and logical errors
- Add coaching skill to the myriad of problem-solving approaches in use
- Build mutual empathy and respect between the owners of the respective disciplines

Changing the conventional approach to coaching in this way significantly increases the quantity of coaching, as coaching is applied non-hierarchically in all directions that arise every day in informal conversations, meetings etc.

It also develops appreciation of the limits to analysis and the value of experimentation. This involves multiple inexpensive experiments rather than being content to implement the analytically "best" solution (often not the best when it meets reality).

Constructive Feedback

The approach in this pillar is to debunk the idea that constructive feedback is negative to encourage quick, non-judgmental conversations to "nip any issues in the bud".

Escalation

The approach here focuses on the skills to both informally and formally escalate while maintaining the relationship with the person.

Quality and quantity

The Quality x Quantity section emphasises that while the quality of the conversation matters so does the number of conversations taking place. Many trends in business, from increasing spans of control to giving front-line leaders lots of administrative work go in the exact opposite direction.

In summary, leadership is a contact sport and the amount of contact matters. Leaders can't do it well in the settings many of them find comfortable such as email or via corporate communications.

Many thanks to Frank Devine for giving permission for use of his materials in this book.

Having looked at creating a continuous improvement culture and leadership system to sustain it, let's cover some key remaining tasks.

Key Tasks Are:

- Create communications and action plan
- Train leaders in leadership standard work
- Create leadership standard work routine

Key Outputs include:

- Communications and action plan
- Leadership standard work routine

Step 8 Process Validation and improvement

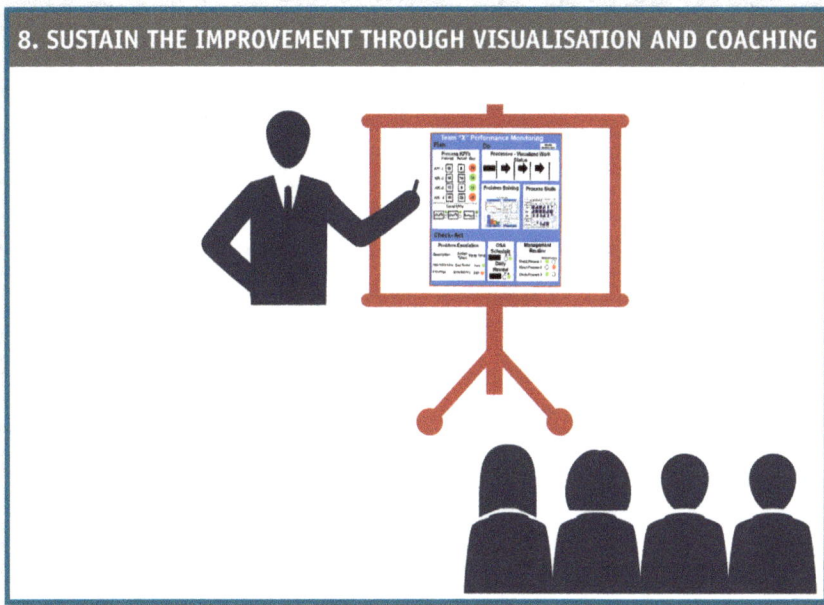

8. SUSTAIN THE IMPROVEMENT THROUGH VISUALISATION AND COACHING

Visualisation of the process helps create an environment for continuous improvement

As mentioned earlier, the key to delivering and sustaining improvements after the workshop has finished is through the check and coaching process from leadership. To enable the check and coaching, process visualisation must be in place. The visualisation must be driven by the team, for the team to help it in its daily work, to drive continuous improvement and to share information. The information that is shared is for the team to use and "others" – these are leaders who should be able to see the status of the process and any improvement actions at an instance and should also be able to see the reaction to delays or non-standard performance. Using visualisation in this provide the tool for the process to become "self-healing" – problems are identified immediately and tackled at the workplace by the team.

Validation of process improvement actions and process performance are the 2 key elements that will help support deployment and continued improvement. Improvement actions must be completed alongside the day job so close monitoring is needed to ensure completion. Monitoring performance is a way of checking that the actions are having a positive impact as well as identifying further areas for improvement

Leadership's role is to validate the process performance through "go-see" and coaching process performance at the workplace. This is enhanced if leaders become expert in Devine's accountability coaching process outlined earlier.

Another method of coaching is the Kata method described by Mike Rother - which is detailed in his book: Toyota Kata. In brief this involves asking the 5 structured Kata questions:

1. What is the target condition?
2. What is the actual condition now?
3. What obstacles do you think are preventing you from reaching your target condition? – which one are you working on now?

4. What is your next step? – what do you expect?

5. How quickly can we go and see what we have learned from taking that step?

Using these questions as a framework for coaching combined with Devine's Cathedral model provide an excellent combination of coaching and feedback.

The key elements of a team's process visualisation board

It is easy for leaders to get a little too enthusiastic about a team's visualisation board. They specify the content based on what they think is important and not what is important to the team. Typically, the team ends up with high level metrics and performance that they have little chance of influencing. These boards are quickly consigned to the graveyard and the concept of team boards and visualisation ends up with a bad name.

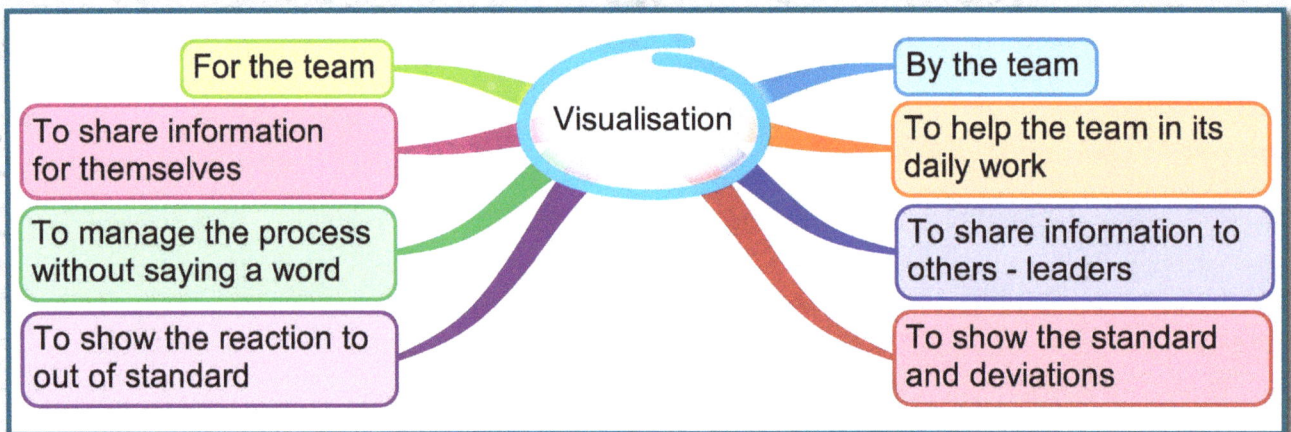

Developed for one of the author's workshops

As can be seen in the mind map, a visualisation board needs to be created and owned by a team. It needs to focus on the things that are important to the team, things they can influence and communicate to themselves and others – important elements of their process and its performance.

At one site of a global company that we visited; the regional supply chain leader had installed a team board for his local team. A huge whiteboard which had been consigned to a corner of the office and was now collecting dust. The local team had not been involved with its creation, nor agreed with the content so consequently was only filled in and used when the supply chain director visited!

A HR process visualisation example

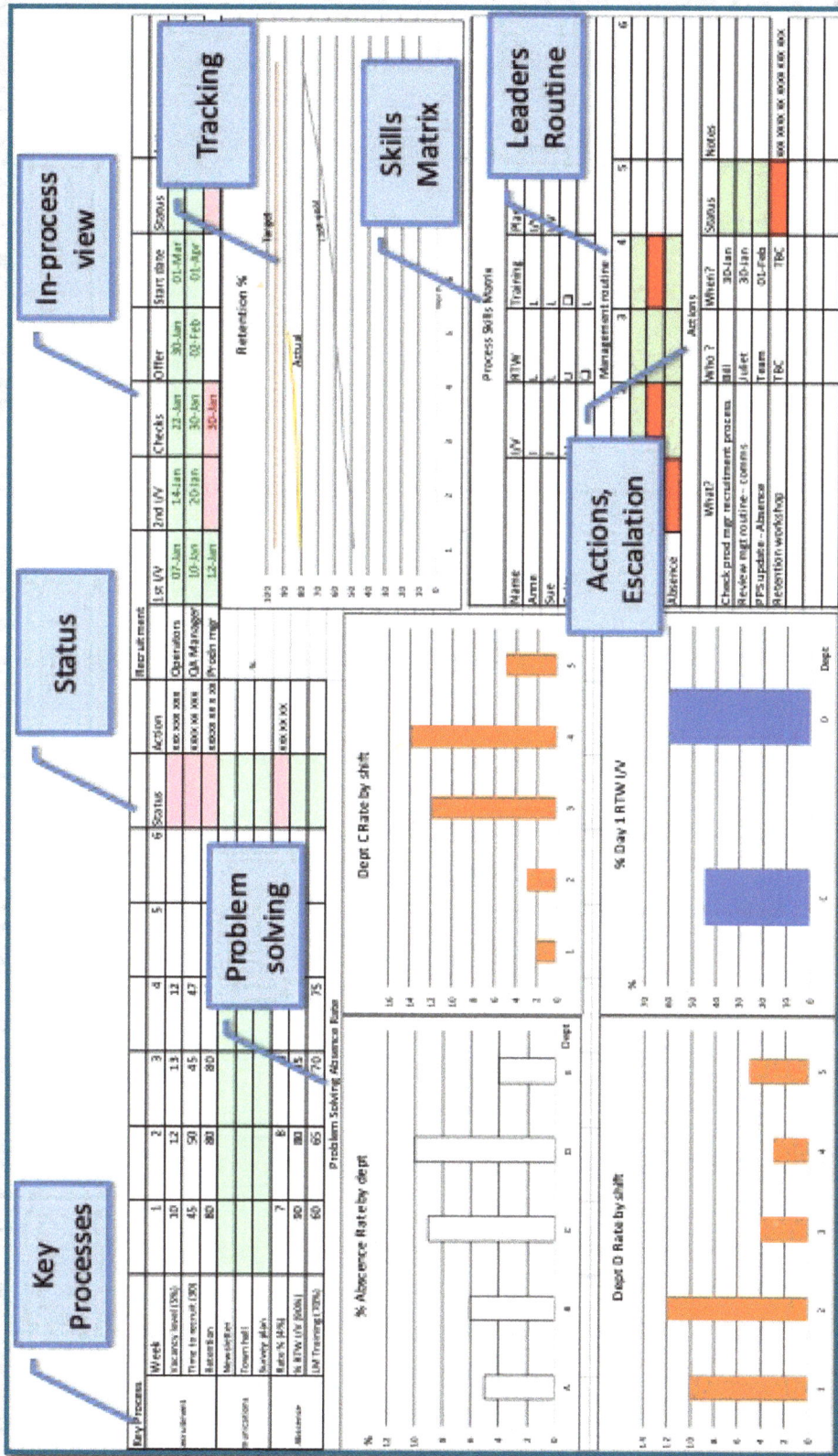

Labels on diagram: Key Processes, Status, In-process view, Tracking, Skills Matrix, Leaders Routine, Problem solving, Actions, Escalation

Here is an example of process visualisation by a HR team. They have identified their key processes – recruitment, communications, and absence, and identified their performance and status. Each element of non-standard performance has a red status and an escalation action to rectify the performance. The recruitment process has been identified as critical and is detailed step by step as a result. The performance for each process is shown visually and the first steps of problem solving for retention have been started. The action plan covers performance improvement and improvement actions. A skills matrix has been added to visualise the competence gaps on each process.

The main elements for a team's visual display board are:

- Key processes for the team are identified
- Improvement objectives are clear and linked to CI Plan
- Latest 8 Step information for the process they are currently improving is displayed
- The action plan status is visible for improvements they are making
- Current performance improvement KPI's for the process the team is changing
- Team Improvement activity / review schedule – for meeting or time out for making improvements
- Management routines are clear to support improvement activity

Visualising and focusing on key processes aligned to the business will help to achieve overall business objectives.

The visualisation needs to focus on how processes are working today? And what are the problems we need to solve now? The status of teamwork activities to review daily if possible – how did we do yesterday/what do we need to do today - so that the team can "see" its work and react accordingly.

KPIs should be derived from the future state process design and be aligned to process customer value. The visualisation should also include current day-to-day performance problems which need to be tracked and escalated to the next level when they can't be solved by the team. Ensuring there are the right of amount of people skilled in understanding and operating the process is crucial, so a RACI and skills matrix should be included.

Management validation cycles to check on performance and people working to the standard should be clearly defined and be included so that expectations of leaders are clear.

The drive for the daily meetings should be keeping the current processes performing to standard

The benefits of visualisation enable the team to "see" its work and react accordingly. Visualisation also gives structure to the team's improvement activity and leadership can ask questions about status and how they can support them. Leadership's role in addition to coaching is recognition on a regular basis.

Key Tasks are:

- Create a visual board to manage the process. Include KPIs, appropriate graphs and charts to show if the process performance is performing to target
- Develop a reaction process for non-standard performance
- Include the leadership standard work routine developed in step 7

Key Outputs include:

- Develop and implement the process visualisation board
- Create a check and reaction system for the process

Conclusion

Lean improvement classically starts in the factory, however as mentioned at the start of this manual, many issues in the factory are caused by decisions and actions taken in the office – in a different place and quite often at a time before you see the effects in the factory. So, it's just as important to ensure that the office processes are included in any Lean improvement initiative.

Business process improvement really focuses of lead time improvement – with its associated quality benefits. If there's a performance gap to close, then it's likely that 8 step practical problem solving will be required. Be careful though! A process improvement activity could require problem solving in parts of the process and in a similar way problem solving may require process improvement to help close the gap.

The 8 step Business Process Improvement method provides a structure and method for improving business processes. It takes the team through the series of steps required to improve a process through a reduction in lead time and improvement in quality.

It does require time and effort to align the team and stakeholders, prepare for the mapping, run the event, create an action plan, develop visualisation and leadership standard work to sustain and continually improve the future state process.

So, planning and preparation is everything, but the rewards will be there in the end.

References

Bicheno J. and Holweg M. The New Lean Toolbox. 5th Edition 2016

Brophy, A (2012) FT Guide to Lean: How to Streamline Your Organisation, Engage Employees and Create a Competitive Edge. Financial Times Series

Devine, F (2016) Demystifying Leadership-Setting Leaders Up for Success. Lean Management Journal.

Devine F (2016) When employees create their own high-performance culture: the rapid, mass engagement process. Lean Management Journal

Devine F (2016) The rapid, mass engagement process—part two. Lean Management Journal

Devine, F and Bicheno, J (2019) Creating Employee 'Pull' for Improvement: Rapid, Mass Engagement for Sustained Lean. Proceedings from the 6th Lean Educators Conference 2019. Springer

Dimancescu D. and Dwenger K. World Class New Product Development. 1996

Hopp W. and Spearman M. Factory Physics. 2000

Rother M. Toyota Kata. 2010

Seddon J Freedom from Command and Control. 2003

Index